Preface

A LL WORKS WHICH PURPORT to describe contemporary situations inevitably become dated and, as a result, they gradually lose their value as anything but historical documents. This monograph attempts to present a picture of Ecuador in the first half of 1976, noting the historical trends which have affected the country since the Second World War, and attempting short-term projections into the future. Since 'development' has so many different meanings and connotations, it might help the reader if, at the outset, I provide my own definition. I consider 'development' simply as 'change through time'. In using the term, there is no implication that changes are either good or bad. Thus, in some fields, development has been beneficial to Ecuador, whilst in others development has been prejudicial to the long-term future of the country. The interpretation of development as a purely economic process is strongly opposed. Development is viewed as a complex process with economic, social, political, spatial, and other dimensions.[1] The view of development as 'the diffusion of modernization' is equally opposed because of its strongly 'ethnocentric' implications that the good things of life are based in Western Europe and North America and diffuse from those areas to the remainder of the non-communist world. Instead, the development of Ecuador is interpreted as a process of changing dependency relations within a world system centred on North America, Western Europe, and Japan.[2] Ecuador is seen as a small nation which, though capable of independent action, has generally been dependent upon external changes and interventions in determining the major patterns of its own development. In the framing and execution of their own

---

[1] The multidimensional nature of development is well presented in Brookfield (1975), Seers (1972), and UNCSD (1972).

[2] Useful introductions to the enormous literature on dependency can be found in Cardoso (1972), Chilcote (1974), Cockcroft, Frank and Johnson (1970), Girling (1973), Mattelart (1970), Quijano (1971), and Schuurman (1974). The concept of dependency is employed by many authors with a wide variety of political leanings and disciplinary backgrounds. As a major concept in social science, dependency has the same virtues and vices as all other important concepts (eg 'scale economies', 'class', and 'hierarchy'). It is an important principle which clarifies many problematical areas, but its all-embracing character means that it is imprecise, and that it varies considerably in importance according to the conditions of the situation under consideration.

iii

policies, the nation's economic, political, and technocratic elites have generally relied upon external stimuli and initiatives, and have often also relied upon external resources.

Ecuador's internal elites acquire most of their tastes, desires, and ideas from abroad, and particularly from North America and Western Europe. In many senses, the elites are more closely linked to Miami, New York and Paris than to the remoter parts of their own country. Furthermore, most wealthy Ecuadorians are more willing to invest abroad, and even to emigrate, than to commit their resources within the country. The investments that they do make are frequently short-term and speculative or exploitative in character. Thus, the external dependency of Ecuador is accompanied by a process of internal domination in which the majority of resources are owned by, and used for the benefit of, a small minority of the national population.[3] This minority is closely dependent upon, and is often directly associated with, foreign interests. The majority of the Ecuadorian population has little voice in government or private enterprise decision-making, and may be used as a source of cheap labour or electoral votes, or may simply be excluded from the benefits of development as an economically unnecessary marginal population. It is not an uncommon view amongst Ecuadorian economic and social elites that economic development must be achieved 'in spite of' rather than 'through the participation of' the broad mass of the Ecuadorian population.

Ecuadorian development is basically a dependent, capitalist development process similar to that in most other Ibero-American countries. This process is characterized by: a high degree of internal inequality; a dominant, materialistic western culture; a high level of foreign indebtedness; a reliance upon imported technology, entrepreneurship, and expertise; the penetration of multinational corporations; and, at times, strong external intervention in internal political processes (see eg Griffin, 1969; Stavenhagen, 1974). The special, though far from unique, features of Ecuador's development are mainly related to the country's small size and population, to its particular range of natural resources, and to its relatively low level of European immigration. These factors are important in explaining Ecuador's territorial losses to Colombia and Peru, and the relatively

---

[3] Useful introductions to the concept of internal domination can be found in Aguirre Beltrán (1967), Cotler (1970), González Casanova (1969), Hechter (1975), and Stavenhagen (1974).

DEVELOPMENT AND PLANNING IN ECUADOR

R. J. BROMLEY

Centre for Development Studies
University College of Swansea
University of Wales

Printed March 1977

Copyright R. J. Bromley

ISBN: 0 9500787 5 1

Published by Latin American Publications Fund
Printed by The Hove Printing Company, Hove, Sussex, England

high penetration of entrepreneurs, investment, technology, and industrial products from other Latin American countries in the Ecuadorian market.

In this monograph, planning is considered to be a scientific decision-making process which takes account of past and present situations in framing policies for the future, and which coordinates policies so as to ensure that the benefits resulting from each measure are not prejudiced by the results of the other measures. Effective planning requires a close involvement of planners in the implementation of their plans, and a friendly collaboration of different individuals, agencies, and institutions in the execution of the plans. It also requires a continuous process of monitoring and evaluation so as to be able to adjust plans to changing circumstances, and to correct errors in policy specifications during the implementation process. It is legitimate, and, indeed, obvious for the reader to ask what is the connection between development and planning. In some countries, it can fairly be said that the process and pattern of development is planned, and, as a result, the connection between planning and development is an integral part of the system of government. In Ecuador, however, the major features of national development have not been planned by Ecuadorians, and many have not been planned at all. Development and planning are barely connected, but they do have a major common characteristic, dependency; both are essentially implanted from outside the country. For either to become effective and beneficial to the great majority of Ecuadorians, the growth of a real spirit of national independence is an essential prerequisite.

This monograph is based upon various periods spent in Ecuador between 1967 and 1976, totalling about two-and-a-half years, together with longer periods spent studying Ecuador in Britain. During this time, I have developed a deep affection for Ecuador and its people, an affection which is the strongest national affiliation that I am likely to possess in my life. The good features of this monograph can be attributed to the wisdom of my Ecuadorian friends and to the critical insight of my wife, Rosemary. The bad features reflect the imperfections of my own understanding of Ecuador.

LATIN AMERICAN PUBLICATIONS FUND

Contents

		PAGE
PREFACE	... ...	iii
CONTENTS	... ...	vii
LIST OF TABLES	... ...	viii
LIST OF FIGURES	... ...	ix

CHAPTER I: FOREIGN DEPENDENCE

International relations 2
Cultural dependency 5
Foreign trade and economic integration 6
Technological dependency 17

CHAPTER II: INTERNAL INEQUALITIES

The distribution of income and wealth... 19
Regional disparities 24
Race and class 36

CHAPTER III: POLITICAL CHANGES SINCE 1948

The political context 44
Political change 49
Recent economic changes and their influence on political
power relationships 59

CHAPTER IV: PLANNING IN ECUADOR SINCE 1950

Attitudes to planning and impediments to its effectiveness ... 67
The institutional position of the National Planning Board ... 72
Integral national plans 80
Sectoral planning 88
Regional planning 92
Local planning 101

CHAPTER V: CONCLUSION 103

BIBLIOGRAPHY 108

List of Tables

TABLE   PAGE

1 The composition of Ecuador's exports between 1971 and 1975, by value 8

2 The most significant changes in Ecuador's economy between 1971 and 1975 9

3 Destinations of Ecuador's exports by countries and groups of countries, 1968–1973, calculated as percentages of the total fob value of exports 11

4 Sources of Ecuador's imports by countries and groups of countries, 1968–1973, calculated as percentages of the total cif value of imports 12

5 The distribution of national income amongst the economically active population in 1966 21

6 The development of land tenure between 1954 and 1968 ... 23

7 Population distribution, density and growth rates by regions, 1950–1972 27

8 Rural-Urban disparities in education and housing conditions in 1974 31

9 Population, public sector accounts, tax revenue, and public sector bank credits, by provinces 35

10 Presidents of Ecuador, 1948–1976 50

11 Government and private investment specified in the Third National Plan, 1964–1973 81

12 Government investment specified in the Fourth National Plan, 1970–1973 83

13 Government and private investment specified in the Fifth National Plan, 1973–1977 84

List of Figures

FIGURE   PAGE

1 Ecuador's territorial claims   3

2 Ecuador's mainland provinces and provincial capitals   ... 16

3 Roads and principal towns and cities in 1975   25

4 Population distribution in 1974   29

5 The structure of the National Planning Board in 1973   ... 77

6 Major regional and local development projects   91

CHAPTER I

Foreign Dependence

ALTHOUGH ECUADOR IS ONE OF Latin America's most important oil exporters and the world's largest exporter of bananas, it is, by most standards, a small and little-known country. With an area of about 264,000 square kilometres,[4] Ecuador is slightly larger than West Germany or Great Britain, but the total population recorded in the June 1974 census was only 6.5 millions (OCN, 1974, 2).[5] Evenly spread over the national territory, this would give a population density of about 25 persons per square kilometre. In reality, however, the population is concentrated in a number of widely-separated clusters in the Andean highlands and Pacific coastal lowlands, while the eastern lowland areas and the Galapagos Islands are only very sparsely populated.

Estimates of the gross domestic product (gdp) in 1974 (IADB, 1976, 378) show Ecuador to have an average of 429 US dollars per capita. A figure such as this fails to convey anything of the great disparity between Ecuador's few rich citizens and her many poor ones, but it does provide a useful international comparative index of the per capita production of goods and services. The Ecuadorian level is one of the lowest in Latin America, the only countries below Ecuador being Bolivia, Haiti, Honduras and Paraguay (IADB, 1976, 378). In gdp per capita terms, Ecuador is somewhat poorer than either of her two neighbours, Peru and Colombia, and has little more than a quarter of the wealth of Venezuela and Argentina, the two richest Latin American nations. The Ecuadorian level is three to four times higher than the per capita levels in the poorest African and Asian countries, but only one-seventh of the British level and one-sixteenth of the United States level (UNDESA, 1975, 650–2).

---

4 This is the area of Ecuador according to her internationally recognized frontiers. It does not include Ecuador's unilateral territorial claims from Peru.

5 This census excludes Ecuador's nomadic population and a few thousand settled inhabitants in small areas where the census takers were rejected by the population. The inclusion of these inhabitants would increase the national population by about 60,000.

1

International relations

Ecuador became independent in 1830 with the break-up of the Federation of Gran Colombia, established at the end of the Spanish colonial period in 1822. Ecuador originated from the Spanish Colonial *Real Audiencia* of Quito, but since independence substantial areas of this *Audiencia* have been lost to Ecuador's larger and more populous neighbours, Colombia and Peru. Much of what is now southern Colombia was once governed from Quito, and was taken by Colombia through diplomatic manoeuvres and military force in the 1820s and 1830s. Further areas were ceded to Colombia in 1916. Ecuador's territorial losses to Colombia occurred so long ago that no grudge remains on Ecuador's part, and relations with Colombia have been amicable for almost all of the last 100 years. In the case of Peru, however, territorial disputes and long-standing grudges have persisted to the present day. Since independence, Peru and Ecuador have disputed large areas to the east of the Andes and limited areas around Tumbez on the Pacific coast. Peru has gained control over almost all of the disputed areas, first through the gradual penetration of Peruvian colonists, and then through a military victory over Ecuador in 1941 (see Ireland, 1938, 175–206 and 219–30; Zook, 1964; Maier, 1969a). Peru's invasion of Ecuador in 1941 was quickly terminated by North American political pressure, leading to the signing of the Rio de Janeiro Protocol in 1942, in which Ecuador effectively conceded most of Peru's territorial claims. There is still considerable bitterness against Peru in Ecuador, not only because Peru used military force rather than negotiation as a means to gain territory from Ecuador, but also because Peru chose to make war at a time when Ecuador was militarily and economically weak, and was ruled by a politically corrupt and dictatorial regime. In 1960, Ecuador's government unilaterally rejected the Rio Protocol and laid claim to all the territory she had claimed before the war with Peru. Thus, all maps published in Ecuador must show national frontiers according to Ecuador's official claims, almost doubling Ecuador's size and including such important Peruvian towns as Tumbez, Jaén and Iquitos. Because of her small size, Ecuador is unlikely ever to be able to regain the lost territories on her own, but the maintenance of her territorial claims and the substantial grudge borne against Peru mean that relations with her southern neighbour are far less friendly than with Colombia. The

2

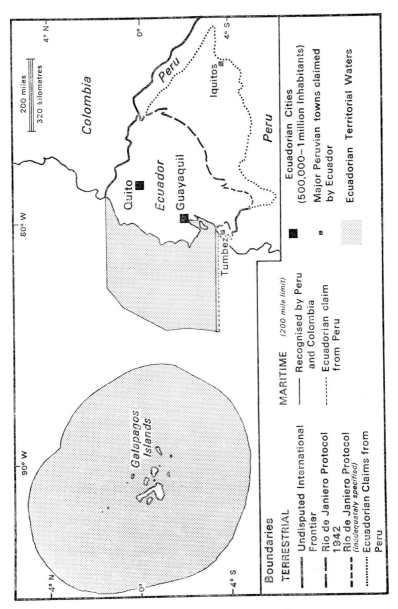

FIGURE 1: ECUADOR'S TERRITORIAL CLAIMS

3

territorial dispute east of the Andes has been made much more important since 1967 by the discovery of substantial oil reserves in north-eastern Ecuador relatively close to the Colombian and Peruvian borders, and by parallel Peruvian discoveries in the areas claimed by Ecuador but internationally recognized to be in Peru. Since the discovery of oil, the Ecuadorian government has been much more cautious in voicing its territorial claims, and relations between Ecuador and Peru have been relatively cordial, reflecting Ecuadorian fears that further conflicts might lead to the loss of their oilfields in the eastern lowlands.

It would be unfair to discuss Ecuador's territorial losses without mentioning one outstanding foreign policy success, her claim to, and defence of, a 200-mile maritime territorial limit. This limit was first proclaimed jointly by Chile, Peru and Ecuador in 1952, and these three countries have pioneered an extension of territorial waters which is being adopted by an increasing number of countries, and which is continuing to gather support (see Teitelboim, 1970). It is common-place in Ecuador now to talk of the country's five natural regions: the coastal lowlands (*costa*), the Andean highlands (*sierra*), the eastern or Amazonian lowlands (*oriente*), the Galapagos Islands, and the territorial waters. Ecuador has shown considerable firmness in the defence of her maritime claims, capturing and fining hundreds of US fishing boats in what has come to be known as the 'Tuna War', and resisting US government pressure to abandon her maritime claims.

The international prestige acquired by Ecuador in her claims to, and defence of, a 200-mile maritime limit, has been further increased by her joining the Organization of Petroleum-Exporting Countries (OPEC) in 1973. Membership of OPEC has allied Ecuador with the most economically powerful group of Third World nations, and has given her a new consciousness of the possible role that she can play in the world economic and political system. Ecuador, however, is the second smallest oil producer amongst the 13 OPEC members, and is clearly seen by the major oil companies as a potential weak link in the OPEC alliance. In the first half of 1975, the Texaco-Gulf consortium, which produces and exports most of Ecuador's oil, drastically reduced exports in a bid to force the Ecuadorian government to reduce oil prices or to reduce taxes on oil exports (see *Nueva* No 21, July 1975, 48–57). This economic pressure paid off in July 1975 when taxes on oil exports to the main consuming areas of the world were

4

reduced. It is clear now that Ecuador has lost the initiative in her relations with foreign oil companies, and that a more conciliatory policy has been adopted in the hope of attracting new oil-exploration investment.

Politically, Ecuador has generally followed a middle-of-the-road or right-wing model, remaining firmly beneath the US political and economic umbrella which has covered most of Latin America throughout the last century. Ecuador has never been invaded by the United States, like Nicaragua, Cuba or the Dominican Republic, but the United States has persistently intervened in Ecuador's internal affairs, and it is no coincidence that most of Agee's (1975) revelations about the activities of the US Central Intelligence Agency concern Ecuador. Ecuador has had many revolutions in its history, but none of these revolutions has been truly radical; indeed, most have been decidedly reactionary. The Ecuadorian government has generally followed a 'dependent capitalist model'. Successive governments have relied heavily upon foreign investment, foreign loans and foreign technical expertise, to encourage Ecuadorian economic growth. Moderate economic growth has resulted, but this growth might well be considered 'growth without development' (see Clower, Dalton, Harwitz and Walters, 1966), because it fails to break the ties of dependency which are associated with underdevelopment.

Cultural dependency

Although Ecuador's cultural roots lie in pre-Columbian America and colonial Spain, the dominant contemporary cultural influences come from North America, Western Europe and other Latin American countries. By far the strongest influence is that of the United States, Ecuador's principal trading partner, the main focus of Ecuadorian emigration overseas, and the main source of foreign visitors to Ecuador. Ecuador's cultural dependency is strongly shown by preferences for North American and European goods, fashions, food and music, and the adoption of English-language names for Ecuadorian-produced goods, and for many shops, restaurants and

5

hotels. Thus, for example, the two major brands of cigarettes which are produced in Ecuador from locally-grown tobacco are called 'Full Speed' and 'Lucky Strike', and the most widely-desired cigarette is 'Marlboro', manufactured in the United States.

Dependence is strongly shown by the widespread belief that imported goods, whatever their origin or brand, must be better than locally-produced goods. This belief is so strong that a common trick in the textile industry is to stick 'Made in Colombia' labels on Ecuadorian textiles so as to be able to sell them at a higher price. Although Ecuador is less Americanized than Venezuela or Panama, it has shown considerably less cultural independence and nationalism than such Latin American nations as Mexico and Peru. Ecuador's cultural dependence has encouraged reliance on foreign investment and expertise, the unnecessary import of foreign-produced goods and technologies, conspicuous consumption by local elites, and the emigration of local technicians. It has acted as a disincentive to domestic industrialization and to domestic entrepreneurship, and has encouraged Ecuador's successive governments to copy development styles and strategies from North America and Europe rather than to try to devise strategies more suitable to local conditions.

Foreign trade and economic integration

Ecuador's relatively small population and low per capita production and income pose special problems for her economic development.[6] The small size of the domestic market means that many industries and specialized services cannot operate with the scale economies available in countries with a larger home demand. Thus, a continuing large-scale importation of sophisticated manufactured goods like machinery and motor vehicles is almost inevitable. The great majority of local industries need the protection of tariff barriers against cheaper foreign competition, yet in a country where contraband trading seems endemic, attempts to foster local industry by tariff protectionism are often doomed to failure. Kuznets (1960, 14–23) has shown how, in order

---

[6] On the characteristics and problems of small-scale economics, see the essays in Robinson (1960) and Selwyn (1975).

to maintain equivalent living standards, a nation with a small population must engage in a relatively larger amount of foreign trade than a nation with a larger population, and is, therefore, especially susceptible to changes in the terms and volume of international trade. Furthermore, Kuznets shows that small nations are generally forced to depend for their livelihood on a very limited range of export products.

Ecuador's exports have always been predominantly made up of primary products, and have usually been dominated by only one to three different products. In the nineteenth and early twentieth centuries, the dominant export was cocoa. In the 1920s and 1930s, coffee and cocoa jointly dominated Ecuadorian exports. During the Second World War, they were supplemented by rice, balsa wood and other products required for the war. After the war, coffee and cocoa continued as important exports, joined by Panama hats,[7] a brief fashion, and by bananas, the basis for the export economy of the 1949–1972 period. During the 1950s and 1960s, Ecuador's export economy was dependent upon four tropical agricultural products from the coastal lowlands — bananas, coffee, cocoa and sugar, which together made up almost 90% of her total exports in the period 1968–1970 (BCE, 1971, 209–11).

The export economy of the 1950s and 1960s, based mainly upon bananas, and secondly upon coffee, cocoa and sugar, has been drastically altered since 1972, when major oil exports began from the Texaco-Gulf fields in north-eastern Ecuador. In the last months of 1972, crude oil was already Ecuador's principal export, and the importance of oil increased dramatically in 1973 and 1974 with the worldwide increases in oil prices. The total value of Ecuador's exports in us dollars virtually quintupled from 1971 to 1974, and in 1974, oil made up almost three-fifths of total exports (Table 1). The importance of the economic transformation of the 1971–75 period can hardly be exaggerated. In this time, Ecuador was converted from a relatively stagnant, 'low pressure' economy into a dynamic 'high pressure' economy. Exports of traditional products generally increased slowly over this period, so that with the addition of oil, there was a major inflow of foreign exchange. Oil has also made Ecuador a much more attractive prospect for foreign investors and aid donors, so that the

---

[7] Panama hats have no connection with Panama beyond the fact that they are usually exported by sea through the Panama Canal. They are made by Ecuadorian artisans in the provinces of Azuay, Cañar and Manabí, from the *toquilla* fibre grown in Ecuador.

7

TABLE 1

THE COMPOSITION OF ECUADOR'S EXPORTS BETWEEN 1971 AND 1975, BY VALUE

(in millions of US dollars, fob)

Source: BCE (1975, 10, and 1976, 10)

		Crude oil	Bananas and banana products[1]	Cocoa and cocoa products[2]	Coffee	Sugar and molasses[3]	Other significant agricultural products[4]	Marine products[5]	Balsa and other timber[6]	Main manufactured exports[7]	Others	TOTAL[8]
1971	No	1	102	30	36	14	4	15	4	4	7	217
	%	0.5	47.0	13.8	16.8	6.5	1.9	6.7	1.7	1.8	3.3	100.0
1972	No	60	110	30	43	17	6	17	4	5	9	301
	%	19.9	36.5	9.8	14.1	5.7	2.0	5.6	1.5	1.8	3.1	100.0
1973	No	250	110	36	67	14	12	24	6	8	17	544
	%	45.9	20.2	6.6	12.2	2.5	2.3	4.5	1.2	1.4	3.2	100.0
1974	No	615	115	126	67	45	13	29	8	13	20	1,050
	%	58.5	10.9	12.0	6.4	4.2	1.3	2.8	0.8	1.2	1.9	100.0
1975	No	516	144	71	64	16	10	37	9	13	18	897
	%	57.5	16.1	7.9	7.1	1.8	1.1	4.1	1.0	1.4	2.0	100.0

1 Banana products made up less than 1% of this category in all years.
2 Cocoa products made up between 15% and 19% of this category in each year.
3 Molasses and *panela* (crude brown sugar) made up between 1.7% and 11.6% of this category in each year.
4 In order of importance: vegetable oils, Manila hemp, pyrethrum, tea and flowers.
5 Mainly tuna, sardines, fishmeal and shrimps.
6 Balsa made up between 76% and 88% of this category in each year.
7 In order of importance: chemical and pharmaceutical products; Panama hats; and domestic electrical goods.
8 Raw totals are not necessarily equal to the totals in this column because of rounding.

8

TABLE 2

THE MOST SIGNIFICANT CHANGES IN ECUADOR'S ECONOMY BETWEEN
1971 AND 1975

	1971	1972	1973	1974	1975
Imports (in millions of US dollars, cif)*	257	249	346	618	824
Exports (in millions of US dollars, fob)*	217	301	544	1,050	897
Net international monetary reserves at year's end (millions of sucres)*	621	3,199	5,650	8,486	6,139
Money supply at year's end, in thousands of millions of sucres† ...	6.0	7.3	9.6	13.1	n a
Reserve money supply at year's end, in thousands of millions of sucres†	4.3	5.8	7.5	9.3	n a
Retail price index in mid-year (all items) 1970 = 100†	108	117	132	163	189
Retail price index in mid-year (food) 1970 = 100†	106	118	142	188	224
gdp in purchaser's values at constant prices (base year 1970) in thousand million sucres‡	35.9	38.0	44.9	51.0	53.7
Total credit given by the national banking system, in thousand million sucres*	12.6	14.4	17.5	25.4	33.1
Percentage growth in gdp during each year (US dollar values at 1973 prices)§	5.4	8.6	17.6	11.7	c 5.3

* Source: BCE (1976a). Imports and exports are provisional figures based upon permits issued.
† Source: UN (1975, 212–29).
‡ Source: BCE (1976c).
§ Source: IADB (1976, 4) for 1971–4. BCE (1976c) for 1975.
n a Not available.
One us dollar = approximately 25 sucres.

inflow of investment and loan funds has also greatly increased. The
principal changes which occurred between 1971 and 1975 are illustrated
by the data presented in Table 2. During this period, there was a
striking increase in Ecuador's exports and foreign exchange reserves,
giving an initial high positive trade balance which has subsequently

declined as imports have increased to catch up with exports. At the same time, inflation accelerated rapidly, paralleling increases in the money supply and world inflationary trends.

Just as Ecuador has traditionally been dependent on a few primary products for almost all of her exports, her foreign trade has traditionally been oriented primarily towards North America and Western Europe. Though Japan and a few Latin American countries have increased somewhat in importance over the last decade, there is still little choice of purchasers for most Ecuadorian products or of suppliers for some of Ecuador's imports. This situation is illustrated by Tables 3 and 4, which show the direction of Ecuador's trade from 1968 to 1973. In every year of this six-year period, the more developed capitalist countries (North America, Western Europe, Japan, Australia and New Zealand) supplied more than 77% of Ecuador's imports, and bought at least 73% of her exports. In each year, the USA alone took between 34% and 43% of Ecuador's exports, and supplied between 32% and 44% of her imports.

It has often been argued that the special economic problems of small nations are best solved by the formation of international free trade associations and the development of multinational groups for economic integration. In 1961, Ecuador joined the Latin America Free Trade Association (LAFTA), an organization intended to increase the volume of trade between its members. Since 1967, the member countries of LAFTA have been as follows: Mexico, Colombia, Venezuela, Brazil, Uruguay, Argentina, Chile, Paraguay, Bolivia, Peru and Ecuador. In spite of several major tariff reductions, however, the LAFTA countries only accounted for 9.8% of Ecuador's exports and 12.4% of her imports in the period 1965–70. Dissatisfaction with LAFTA's performance (see Dell, 1966, 105–10; Griffin, 1969, 247–9) and the desire for a closer and more effective form of economic integration led Colombia, Ecuador, Peru, Bolivia and Chile to form the Andean Group in 1969.* Venezuela subsequently joined the Group three-and-a-half years after its foundation. While remaining within LAFTA, the six Andean Group countries are carrying common tariff reductions through more rapidly and are attempting to adopt common economic policies. Along with Bolivia, Ecuador has been allowed a special protected status within the Andean Group to assist her to develop without being swamped

---

* Chile's membership effectively lapsed in October, 1976.

TABLE 3

DESTINATIONS OF ECUADOR'S EXPORTS BY COUNTRIES AND GROUPS OF COUNTRIES, 1968–1973, CALCULATED AS PERCENTAGES OF THE TOTAL FOB VALUE OF EXPORTS

Source: BCE (1975, 292–9)

	1968	1969	1970	1971	1972	1973
MORE DEVELOPED COUNTRIES ...	88.9	87.4	88.7	85.9	84.1	74.8
NORTH AMERICA	38.8	39.7	43.3	42.2	43.0	50.9
USA	38.6	39.5	42.6	41.7	34.5	34.7
Canada	0.2	0.2	0.7	0.5	3.3	1.0
Caribbean oil ports[1]	0.0	0.0	0.0	0.0	5.2	15.2
WESTERN EUROPE	26.9	26.2	21.8	21.1	19.9	16.2
United Kingdom	0.2	0.2	0.2	0.2	0.2	2.2
West Germany	9.8	11.7	9.3	11.3	8.5	6.6
France	1.5	1.7	1.8	1.2	0.8	1.2
Italy	8.4	5.1	3.3	1.8	2.3	0.2
Low countries	5.6	5.9	5.7	5.4	7.2	4.6
Other countries	1.4	1.6	1.5	1.2	0.9	1.4
JAPAN	12.1	12.3	17.9	13.8	15.3	5.1
AUSTRALIA AND NEW ZEALAND	0.1	0.4	0.6	0.5	0.8	0.6
COMMUNIST BLOCK[2]	11.0	8.8	5.1	8.3	5.1	2.0
Eastern Europe	2.3	5.1	4.7	7.1	4.6	1.8
USSR	8.7	3.7	0.4	1.2	0.5	0.2
LESS DEVELOPED COUNTRIES ...	11.1	12.6	11.3	14.1	15.9	25.2
ASIA (excluding Japan)	0.6	1.1	0.0	0.5	1.0	0.4
AFRICA	1.8	0.4	0.2	0.5	0.4	0.6
LATIN AMERICA	8.7	11.1	11.1	13.1	14.5	24.2
LAFTA members outside eventual Andean Group[3]	2.1	3.0	2.9	3.2	2.1	2.9
Eventual Andean Group members[4]	6.3	7.5	7.7	9.6	9.3	13.8
Other countries	0.3	0.6	0.5	0.3	3.1	7.5

1 Netherlands Antilles, and Trinidad and Tobago. These oil ports simply act as refining and transit points in the petroleum trade between Ecuador and the more developed countries.
2 USSR, Poland, East Germany, Czechoslovakia, Hungary, Roumania, Bulgaria, Yugoslavia and Albania.
3 Mexico, Argentina, Uruguay, Brazil and Paraguay.
4 Venezuela, Colombia, Peru, Chile and Bolivia.

TABLE 4

SOURCES OF ECUADOR'S IMPORTS BY COUNTRIES AND GROUPS OF COUNTRIES, 1968–1973, CALCULATED AS PERCENTAGES OF THE TOTAL CIF VALUE OF IMPORTS

Source: BCE (1974, 406–16)

	1968	1969	1970	1971	1972	1973
MORE DEVELOPED COUNTRIES...	90.9	86.0	86.1	83.7	85.8	79.9
NORTH AMERICA	46.8	42.4	45.3	40.1	41.0	34.5
USA ...	43.6	39.2	43.4	38.2	37.9	32.5
Canada	2.6	2.2	1.5	1.3	2.7	1.3
Caribbean oil ports[1] ...	0.6	1.0	0.4	0.6	0.4	0.7
WESTERN EUROPE	36.6	33.3	29.0	26.4	30.8	32.1
United Kingdom	5.6	4.8	4.2	4.2	6.1	4.8
West Germany	11.9	12.1	11.1	11.0	11.1	11.7
France	6.4	2.0	1.8	1.1	1.4	2.8
Italy ...	3.4	3.3	3.1	3.3	2.7	3.0
Low countries	3.4	4.4	3.1	2.5	3.1	3.1
Other countries	5.9	6.7	5.7	4.3	6.4	6.7
JAPAN ...	6.5	8.7	9.3	15.2	12.3	10.9
AUSTRALIA AND NEW ZEALAND	0.2	0.2	0.6	0.3	0.1	0.1
COMMUNIST BLOCK[2]	0.8	1.4	1.9	1.7	1.6	2.3
Eastern Europe	0.8	1.4	1.9	1.7	1.6	2.2
USSR	0.0	0.0	0.0	0.0	0.0	0.1
LESS DEVELOPED COUNTRIES ...	9.1	14.0	13.9	16.3	14.2	20.1
ASIA (excluding Japan)	0.8	1.0	0.8	1.2	1.3	1.6
AFRICA ...	0.1	0.1	0.1	0.1	0.1	0.1
LATIN AMERICA	8.2	12.9	13.0	15.0	12.8	18.4
LAFTA members outside eventual Andean Group[3]...	1.3	1.8	1.9	2.1	3.6	6.9
Eventual Andean Group members[4] ...	6.8	11.0	10.8	12.7	8.6	10.8
Other countries	0.1	0.1	0.3	0.2	0.6	0.7

1 Netherlands Antilles, and Trinidad and Tobago.　These oil ports simply act as refining and transit points in the petroleum trade between Ecuador and the more developed countries.
2 USSR, Poland, East Germany, Czechoslovakia, Hungary, Roumania, Bulgaria, Yugoslavia and Albania.
3 Mexico, Argentina, Uruguay, Brazil and Paraguay.
4 Venezuela, Colombia, Peru, Chile and Bolivia.

by the competition of the four larger and more developed member-countries. In spite of this, however, the benefits of the Andean Group to Ecuador, like those of LAFTA, are likely to prove relatively limited. The main populated areas of the member-countries of the Andean Group are separated by considerable distances, and international transport services are inadequate for large-scale trade. All of the Andean Group nations except Venezuela are relatively poor on a world scale, and all six are basically exporters of primary products and importers of manufactured goods. Ecuador's oil exports to Peru will end once Peru's north-eastern fields come into substantial production in 1977, and oil exports to Chile and Colombia may well also decline rapidly because of Peruvian competition. Ecuador has good prospects of expanding her exports of agricultural products to Colombia, Peru and Chile, and of substituting the purchase of more Colombian and Peruvian industrial products for a small proportion of her existing purchases from North America, Western Europe and Japan. Although trade with the remainder of the Andean Group is increasing,[8] however, it is very unlikely that the predominance of the more developed capitalist countries in Ecuador's foreign trade will be seriously affected.

As a small country, Ecuador is highly dependent upon foreign trade in a few products whose supply, demand and prices are all highly variable. World trade in these products is mainly handled by giant multinational corporations, such as Texaco Oil, Gulf Oil and United Brands, whose annual turnover is far larger than Ecuador's gross domestic product. In addition, of course, these multinational companies are mainly owned by investors in the developed capitalist countries. These countries are the main consumers of Ecuador's products, the main producers of the commodities that Ecuador requires, and the main sources of investment capital for Ecuador's development projects. The result is an almost insoluble situation of economic dependence. Sometimes, the interests of the different advanced, capitalist countries or of the different multinational corporations can be played off against one another, but, in general, Ecuador's powers of independent action are severely limited. Attempts in the

---

[8] A substantial part of the increase in trade with Colombia and Peru is due to the 'legalization' and statistical recording of trade which formerly passed the frontier illegally. The relaxing of regulations and the simplification of border-crossing procedures have persuaded more traders to cross the frontier legally rather than to smuggle goods across illegally.

1960s to stimulate links with the COMECON countries failed miserably, in part because of external and internal political opposition, but more importantly because the USSR and Eastern Europe were unwilling to buy more than a small proportion of the bananas, coffee, cocoa and sugar that Ecuador had to offer, and because Ecuadorians were deeply, and sometimes justifiably, suspicious of manufactured products from communist countries.

Ecuador's dependence on the decisions of the multinational corporations is well illustrated by the cases of bananas and oil. Throughout the 1950s and 1960s, the Ecuadorian economy's fortunes were mainly based on the export of bananas, and even today banana exports are still very important. In general, when production is high in Central America, Ecuador has enormous difficulty in selling her bananas because the large American multinationals prefer to market the produce of their own Central American plantations rather than to buy the more distant Ecuadorian fruit. However, whenever Central American producers are seriously affected by disease or hurricane damage, Ecuador has an easy market for its bananas through the large multinationals. Thus, in a sense, Ecuador is 'marginal' to the world banana market, rapidly filling unsatified demand when the more favourably located producers are unable to maintain their normal output, but losing much of its market as soon as the Central American plantations return to normality (see Preston, 1965; Calzada, 1960, 45). Although Ecuador produces cheap, high-quality bananas, severe restrictions on the areas of plantations have been necessary for many years, and, in most years, far more good bananas have been allowed to rot than have actually been exported. It is perhaps also worth noting that the Ecuadorian banana producer receives only about one-fifth the price for his product that the Ecuadorian exporter receives when that product is exported, and, in turn, that the European or North American consumer pays five to nine times the fob price received by the Ecuadorian exporter (Vera Arrata, 1972, 24).

Dependence on multinational corporations is even more evident in the case of oil. Without the technical expertise and vast resources of foreign corporations, Ecuador would probably never have discovered her north-eastern oilfields. Thus, from the viewpoint of the multinational corporations, foreign capital and expertise have brought great benefits and considerable wealth to Ecuador without great effort or sacrifice on the part of the Ecuadorian government or population. From the viewpoint of many Ecuadorians, however, the multinational corporations and the developed capitalist countries that they represent, are responsible for Ecuador's poverty and for Ecuador's apparent inability to find or exploit her own natural resources. Within the international system, the behaviour of the multinational corporations is perfectly normal and rational, but, from the viewpoint of small and relatively poor countries, it is necessary to question whether the 'rules' of the system are equitable, or whether, in reality, they simply maintain and accentuate the inequalities of the system. Attempts by the Ecuadorian government to weaken their dependence on the multinational oil corporations over the period 1972 to 1974, led by the then Minister of Natural Resources, Captain Gustavo Jarrín Ampudia, came at a very fortunate moment from Ecuador's point of view. During this period, the worldwide balance of power between the governments of the main oil-exporting countries and the multinational oil corporations shifted markedly in favour of the governments. Ecuador took advantage of this worldwide trend to increase her oil revenues, to take control of some of the production and marketing of her own oil, and to tighten controls upon oil and gas exploration (see MRNE, 1973). Initially, the oil companies' only adverse reaction was a virtual stoppage of most exploration activities outside the Texaco-Gulf concessions in the north-east. As the other oil companies gradually withdrew from Ecuador in 1972, 1973 and 1974, Texaco-Gulf's bargaining position with the Ecuadorian government was considerably strengthened. Because the possibility of alternative oil sources outside Texaco-Gulf's control was diminishing, Ecuador's dependence on Texaco-Gulf's expertise was increased. In 1974, pressure on the Ecuadorian government was further facilitated by a falling world demand for oil, and by the growing realization of Ecuador's position as a remote and small-scale producer (see O'Shaughnessy, 1975). Ecuador's 'marginal' position in the world oil market enabled Texaco-Gulf to reduce oil exports and to press for the removal of Jarrín from office and the reduction of taxes on oil exports. Jarrín was finally dismissed at the end of 1974, and taxes were reduced in 1975. Even after this, however, exports were apparently held down by Texaco-Gulf and political pressure was continued in the hope of provoking further tax cuts and an eventual Ecuadorian withdrawal from OPEC (see *Nueva*, No 25, dic 1975, 12–4; No 30, jun 1976, 53; No 32, ago 1976, 8–11).

15

FIGURE 2:

ECUADOR'S MAINLAND PROVINCES AND PROVINCIAL CAPITALS

16

Technological dependency

Ecuador's difficulties with Texaco-Gulf are simply a reflection of her almost total dependence upon foreign technology and her considerable dependence upon foreign capital. In a sense, Ecuador is prepared to accept nothing but the best. Intermediate technology and out-of-date or second-hand equipment and consumer goods are not welcomed by Ecuador's property-owning, industrial and commercial elites. Particularly since oil was discovered in the north-east in 1967, expectations have greatly outrun the capacity to achieve them, and a sense of unreality has prevailed in the choice and design of development projects. The result has been the initiation of too many projects, a rapid increase of imported technology, and a strengthening of dependence upon the developed, capitalist countries.

Perhaps the best illustration of technological dependency is the import-substitution industrialization process which has gradually increased in importance since the early 1960s.[9] More and more factories have been established, usually with foreign capital and/or foreign technical expertise, to assemble consumer goods in Ecuador. Because these goods are assembled in Ecuador, they avoid the main weight of import duties, and hence, can be sold more cheaply than imported finished goods. The great majority of the equipment used in production and the components actually assembled are imported, but these goods carry little or no import duty because they are 'raw materials and equipment for industrial production'. Import substitution has, therefore, led to a decline of imports of finished goods, which at least yield a fairly high tax revenue, and to an increase in the imports of equipment and intermediate goods, which yield little tax revenue. Thus, the national import bill is not substantially reduced, and considerable and continuing payments are required for the right to use foreign technology and the hiring of foreign technical expertise. In the late 1960s, for example, the proportions of imported goods in the raw materials for the following Ecuadorian domestic industries were as follows: heavy metals, 99.9%; paper and cellulose, 97.5%; printing, 97.4%; engineering, 94.5%; electrical machinery and rubber goods,

---

[9] For general discussions of the deficiencies of the import substitution process in Latin American countries, see Griffin (1969, 223–5), Boorstein (1968, 5–7), and Grunwald (1970, 838–40).

17

almost 90.0% (Salgado, 1970, 279). In general, the industries established have generated relatively few jobs in Ecuador because they have adopted highly capital-intensive technologies, and because they usually cater for the demands of the upper and middle classes, groups which are too small to sustain a high level of demand (see Salgado, 1970, 276–88). The import-substitution industrialization process has brought considerable benefits to the international companies which control the supply of technology, equipment and intermediate goods, but it has failed to bring the expected benefits of reduced imports and mass employment for Ecuador.

In reality, however, Ecuador has little choice but to industrialize, and little choice as to how industrialization should be conducted. The Ecuadorian consumer is accustomed to buying foreign goods and deeply distrusts anything which is designed in Ecuador, or which is based on Ecuadorian technology. Foreign technology is seen as a mark of quality and confidence. The research capacity required to develop and sustain genuine Ecuadorian technology is simply not available, and the few people who might contribute to such research are usually earning high salaries in Ecuador or abroad, working for foreign companies. The Ecuadorian government is faced with a very widespread belief, on the part of all social classes, that industrialization is the solution to Ecuador's problems and the road to modernity. A concentration on agriculture, handicrafts and services is seen as impractical and an 'admission of defeat' in the quest for development. Thus, most Ecuadorians are somewhat frustrated devotees of the western, capitalist development model, and not surprisingly, there is little or no support for alternative development models like those being tried out in such countries as China, Tanzania, Somalia and Cuba.

CHAPTER II

Internal Inequalities

S OME DEGREE OF SOCIAL, economic and regional inequality, and of
cultural pluralism, exists in every country in the world. Ecuador
is no exception to this, having a high concentration of wealth and
power in relatively few hands, strong regional and local loyalties, and a
society which combines strong elements of pre-Columbian indigenous
cultures, colonial Spanish culture, and contemporary North American
and Western European culture.

The distribution of income and wealth

Statistical information on the distribution of income and wealth in
Ecuador is, as for most countries, scarce and inaccurate. The general
impression is of a high concentration of both income and wealth in the
hands of a small minority of the population, most of whom are upper-
class urban dwellers with strong foreign links. These wealthy elites
manage most of Ecuador's internal commerce and import-export
trade, and much of the industrial and agricultural production. In
addition, they own most of the farmland and most of the urban real
estate in the country, and have a large share of banking, insurance and
other financial operations.

Ecuador has had no sweeping revolution or reform to break the
long-established hold of her wealthy national elites. These elites
are popularly portrayed as a group of forty inter-related families with
connexions in the church and in the armed forces, and with roots
stretching back to the early colonial period. Such a picture, however,
is a gross over-simplification of reality. Ecuador has a wide variety
of elite groups, and there is little organized elite solidarity. Indeed,
the basic instability of the country and the continual tendency towards
the subdivision and proliferation of institutions point to the intense
subdivision and quarrelsome nature of the nation's elite groups.

19

Though many of the leading highland families have colonial roots and landowner origins, most of the leading coastal families became prominent only during the nineteenth or twentieth centuries, and frequently have merchant origins. Throughout Ecuador's history, the 'hereditary elites' have been joined by new 'self-made men', who have seized particular opportunities to enrich themselves and to push themselves to the top of the socio-economic tree. Their enrichment may lead to the environmental destruction of large areas of their own country, to the exploitation of their fellow Ecuadorians, and to a 'sell-out' to foreign interests, but all these are considered acceptable risks in the quest for personal gain (see Vera Arrata, 1972; *Nueva*, No 21, July 1975, 64–8).

The wealth acquired by individual capitalists through successful entrepreneurial activities is rapidly invested in a wide variety of different places and economic activities, ensuring a lasting family fortune. Traditionally, wealth has been invested in land, but nowadays, urban real estate is the most popular investment. A substantial proportion of the assets of Ecuadorian elites is usually sent abroad, and many of the beneficiaries of the early twentieth-century cocoa boom have settled permanently in Paris and other cities of the more developed countries. Other assets are spread between investments in banking, commerce, industry, agriculture and transport, and some are even devoted to such purposes as sponsoring football clubs and acquiring personal status symbols. Wealthy Ecuadorians usually have strong links with politicians and officers in the armed forces, and political bribery and corruption is commonplace. Thus, wealth may be used to speculate against the national currency or to distort the balance of payments, so generating political pressure against the government. In other cases, it may simply be used to support individual politicians, or to bribe particular groups to make or support a *coup d'état*. Ecuador's elites do make some 'productive entrepreneurial investments', but the majority of these investments are highly personalistic and exploitative in character, seeking a quick profit rather than continuing production and the achievement of scale economies (see Bottomley, 1966; Salgado, 1970, 50–7; Wygard, 1963, 133–6 and 149–52). Their assets are shifted rapidly from one sector of the economy to another as new opportunities arise, contributing to Ecuador's economic instability and 'boom and bust mentality' (see Baraona, 1967; Bromley, 1972; CIDA, 1965, 407–17).

Perhaps the best available income distribution estimates for Ecuador are those for 1966, shown in Table 5. Though these statistics are somewhat dated by population growth and monetary inflation, they probably reflect fairly accurately the contemporary income distribution, with the highest 0.8% of the economically-active population receiving over 20% of total national income, and the lowest half of the economically-active population receiving only about 12% of total national income. Less-comprehensive data for 1970 (Moncada, 1973a, 4) indicate a worsening of this situation, with the lowest 61% of the economically-active population only receiving 12% of the national income. Even in the mid-1970s, the overwhelming majority of Ecuadorian workers still earn under 40 US dollars (1,000 sucres) per month (see eg JNPC, 1973c, 50–7; PREALC, 1975, I–2) while senior company managers and civil servants often earn over 800 US dollars (20,000 sucres) per month. It should also be noted that modern sector wage and salary earners, most of whom earn over 60 US dollars (1,500 sucres) per month, receive the benefits of social security, and are in fact paid for over 14 months work each year, as their 12 monthly salaries are supplemented by two full bonus months' salaries and by an

TABLE 5

THE DISTRIBUTION OF NATIONAL INCOME AMONGST
THE ECONOMICALLY-ACTIVE POPULATION IN 1966

Source: JNPC (1969c, vol 1, 35)

Annual income in sucres	Economically-active population		Percentage of national income received by each income group
	No	%	
Under 3,000	723,200	50.2	12.0
3,000 to 10,000	451,400	31.3	21.1
10,000 to 60,000	249,400	17.2	40.8
60,000 to 100,000	7,300	0.5	5.8
Over 100,000	11,200	0.8	20.3
TOTAL	1,442,500	100.0	100.0

21

additional bonus payment. Such benefits simply enlarge the disparities between the relatively well-off and the poor. The latter are generally self-employed or casual workers and do not qualify for these benefits.

A study of the ownership of limited companies in 1971 revealed that as few as 4,000 people may own over 70% of the investments made in limited companies in Ecuador (INEFOS, 1973, 13). Navarro's (1975) analysis of company ownership in Ecuador demonstrates the high degree of linkage between different companies, and between foreign investors and national elites, as well as the economic predominance of a relatively few families. A substantial number of major companies are owned by Ecuadorian families descended from nineteenth and twentieth century foreign immigrants, generally of European or Middle Eastern origin. Thus, in Guayaquil for example, much of the food-processing industry belongs to families of Italian origin, and several of the largest banks are mainly owned by families of Jewish and Levantine origin.

In a predominantly rural country like Ecuador, perhaps the most important single factor in the distribution of wealth is the ownership of agricultural land. Table 6 shows the high concentration of landholding in a relatively small number of large estates, known as *haciendas* or *latifundia*, and the low percentage of these estates actually under cultivation as revealed by the 1954 and 1968 agricultural censuses. Between 1954 and 1968, the total number of agricultural holdings in Ecuador increased from 344,000 to 633,000 and the proportion of the national territory actually cultivated rose from 7.9% to 14.5%. There was a minor redistribution of land in favour of small and medium scale farmers between the two censuses. This redistribution can mainly be attributed to the impact of Ecuador's Agrarian Reform Law of 1964 and particularly to the abolition of ancient feudal labour relations, giving estate workers formal title to land which they previously held in return for their labour services to the estates (see Benalcázar, 1971; Hurtado and Herudek, 1974, 101). Except for a few estates belonging to public institutions and the church, however, there has been almost no radical land reform in Ecuador comparable to that which has occurred in Mexico and Bolivia, where large estates have been broken up and transferred to the ownership of small peasant farmers and cooperatives. A review in 1970 of Ecuador's very half-hearted attempts at land reform commented that since the 1964 reform law, 'little meaningful reform took place and therefore,

22

TABLE 6

THE DEVELOPMENT OF LAND TENURE BETWEEN 1954 AND 1968

Source: DGEC (1956, 7 and 25, 1969b, 1–3)

Size of holdings in hectares	Percentage of the total number of holdings in each size range		Percentage of the total national farm area in each size range		Average per- centage of each farm actually under cultivation		Percentage of the farms in each size range under owner occupation	
	1954	1968	1954	1968	1954	1968	1954	1968
Under 1.0 ...	26.8	32.6	0.8	1.3	94.3	88.8	79.8	82.4
1.0 to 4.9 ...	46.3	41.7	6.4	8.9	84.1	80.0	58.1	68.7
5.0 to 9.9 ...	10.5	10.8	4.5	6.7	70.0	72.3	64.5	74.6
10.0 to 19.9 ...	6.2	5.7	4.9	7.0	61.5	65.8	71.4	80.4
20.0 to 49.9 ...	5.7	5.2	9.9	14.7	50.2	59.5	82.0	85.8
50.0 to 99.9 ...	2.4	2.5	9.1	14.1	40.1	53.7	82.5	80.0
100.0 to 499.9...	1.7	1.3	19.3	23.8	34.1	50.1	87.5	85.6
500.0 and over	0.4	0.2	45.1	23.5	13.9	38.4	85.5	87.0
All holdings together ...	100.0	100.0	100.0	100.0	34.7	55.0	67.9	75.8

as a practical matter, Ecuador remains in the pre-reform period' (USAID, 1970, 3). A new Agrarian Reform Law was decreed in October 1973, but it has not yet brought any major changes in Ecuador's land tenure structure. A new initiative is urgently needed to achieve an effective agrarian reform, so as to end land speculation and to redistribute large areas to the less-privileged groups of the population.

The high concentration of income and wealth in the hands of relatively few Ecuadorians has very grave consequences for the national patterns of development. While the majority of the popula-tion cannot afford adequate food, clothing or housing, a rich minority are engaged in a process of conspicuous consumption, mainly of imported luxury goods. Substantial proportions of national assets are squandered or sent abroad by the elite groups, and much of the

23

remainder is invested speculatively in land and real estate, contributing little to national production (see Navarro Jimenez, 1975). Because they are relatively few in numbers, and because of their preference for sophisticated foreign products, the elite groups form only a very limited market for national production. Meanwhile, the majority of the population are too poor to consume substantial quantities of anything beyond the most basic agricultural and industrial products. Thus, the existing distribution of income and wealth acts as a disincentive to agricultural and industrial development, and puts a considerable strain upon the national balance of payments. In addition, it diverts investment away from the most potentially productive sectors, and consigns a large part of the labour force to poorly paid and relatively unproductive occupations (see Moncada, 1973a, 28–33; PREALC, 1975). The combination of low incomes and limited economic opportunities for most of the population encourages the persistence of malnutrition, sickness and poor educational performance, perpetuating the vicious circle of poverty which has affected most of Ecuador's population for centuries (see Santos, 1975, 19–33). The redistribution of income and wealth in Ecuador, so as to reduce the disparities between rich and poor, is widely recognized as an essential precondition for effective development (see *eg* GRNE, 1972, 5–6; Hurtado, 1969; Moncada, 1973a; Navarro, 1975, 99–103), but no real progress has been made towards such a redistribution. The present distribution is closely related to Ecuador's economic, political, cultural and technological dependence, and to the low levels of political organization and consciousness amongst large sectors of the Ecuadorian lower classes. Only changes in these relationships can stimulate a major redistribution of wealth and power in Ecuador, narrowing the gap between rich and poor, and increasing the potential for social mobility.

Regional disparities

In spite of Ecuador's fairly small size, regional and local loyalties are exceptionally strong. The land area is divided into four highly-contrasting natural regions: the Galapagos Islands, the coastal

FIGURE 3: ROADS AND PRINCIPAL TOWNS AND CITIES IN 1975

lowlands, the Andean highlands, and the eastern lowlands or *Oriente*. For most of the 287-year-long Spanish colonial period, population was concentrated in the Andean highlands, but since independence the coastal lowlands have been gradually developed for the large-scale production of export crops. An increasing number of temporary and permanent migrants have moved from the over-populated and economically depressed rural areas of the Andean highlands to the coastal lowlands. Thus, the percentage of the national population living in the coastal lowlands has risen from only 12.6% in 1856[10] to 43.5% in 1950 and 54.3% in 1972. Since the nineteenth century, the coastal lowlands have produced the bulk of Ecuador's exports, and hence, the region has tended to be more prosperous and more economically dynamic and susceptible to modernization than the Andean highlands. The highlands have remained poorer and more isolated from international influences, so that the traditional landed aristocracy and the Church have retained their influence to a much greater extent than on the coast, where newer and more commercially oriented merchant and landowner elites have developed. In the nineteenth and early twentieth centuries, there were only two major political parties in Ecuador, the pro-clerical, landowner-dominated Conservative party based in the highlands, and the anti-clerical, merchant-dominated Liberal party based on the coast. This pattern of regional politics still persists, although it has been considerably complicated by the twentieth-century proliferation of new political parties without such sharply defined regional loyalties. The rivalry of the two major regions has been intensified by the development and competition for influence of two widely separated primate cities, Quito, the national capital in the highlands, and Guayaquil, the main port and commercial centre in the coastlands. Influential highlanders have long envied the greater wealth and progress of the coastlands, while the coastal population has a strong dislike of rule by what appears to them a reactionary and parasitic bureaucracy in Quito.

Throughout Ecuador, the widely separated population concentrations tend to be focused on their own central towns and cities, and most of the concentrations form the foci for provincial or cantonal units. Local loyalties are particularly strong in the Andean highlands,

---

[10] Calculated from data in Villavicencio (1858, 164) assuming the number of Indians in the *Oriente* to be 60,000 rather than Villavicencio's highly exaggerated total of 200,000.

TABLE 7

POPULATION DISTRIBUTION, DENSITY AND GROWTH RATES BY REGIONS, 1950–1972[1]

	National total	Galapagos Islands	Coastal lowlands	Andean highlands	Eastern lowlands
1950 census population:					
Total (thousands) ...	3,230	2	1,404	1,754	70
Percentage	100.0	0.1	43.5	54.3	2.1
1972 estimated population:					
Total (thousands) ...	6,622	4	3,455	3,000	163
Percentage	100.0	0.1	52.2	45.3	2.4
Annual percentage rate of population growth 1950–1972	3.3	4.4	4.2	2.5	3.9
Area (thousands of sq km)	264	8	86	77	93
Population density in 1972 (persons per sq km)	25.1	0.5	40.3	39.2	1.7

1 Calculated from data in DGEC (1960 and 1968a) with adjustments to include the nomadic Indian population of the eastern lowlands based on projections of the data in Instituto Interamericano Indigenista (1962, 48). The coastal lowlands are defined as the area west of the Andes and below the 1,500-metre contour; the Andean highlands are defined as the area above the 1,500-metre contour; and the eastern lowlands (*Oriente*) are defined as the area east of the Andes and below the 1,500-metre contour. Adjustments were made to the census data to achieve a fit to these definitions using DGEC (1968b).

where the population is concentrated in isolated valleys and basins which are often separated from one another, and from the coastal and eastern lowlands, by formidable mountain barriers. Each of Ecuador's separate population concentrations has developed over several centuries in relative isolation. Though there have been commercial and migratory flows between the different populated areas of what is now Ecuador for many centuries, these flows have been limited in frequency and volume by the inadequacy of communications links and the formidable nature of the natural barriers separating the different population concentrations. In the twentieth century, physical isolation has been greatly reduced by the introduction of rail and road transport and telecommunications, but these links have not significantly weakened the regional and local loyalties established over several centuries. Ecuador's complex pattern of regional and local loyalties obstructs the development of a spirit of national unity and contributes to the high degree of factionalism, rivalry and mistrust which bedevils Ecuadorian politics. It has contributed to the basic political instability of the country, and has helped to prevent the formation of an effective national system of government and planning.

Mainly for historical reasons, Ecuador's population distribution is in marked disequilibrium with the distribution of resources and economic opportunities. Data on the quantity of potentially cultivable land in Ecuador is very inadequate, but it seems reasonable to suggest that perhaps 75% of the area of the coastal lowlands, 25% of the Andean highlands and 50% of the eastern lowlands would fall into this category.[11]   On the basis of these estimates and the data in Table 7, it can be calculated that 49.5% of Ecuador's potentially cultivable land is in the coastal lowlands, 14.8% in the Andean highlands and 35.7% in the eastern lowlands.   The estimated population distribution for 1972 (Table 7) is as follows: coastal lowlands 52.2%, Andean highlands 45.3%, and eastern lowlands 2.4%.   Of the three major natural regions, only the coastal lowlands exhibit a reasonable balance between population and agricultural resources.   The Andean highlands are seriously overpopulated, and widespread soil erosion has occurred.   In contrast, the agricultural resources of the inaccessible eastern lowlands are almost unused.   In spite of the fact that the proportion of the population living in urban areas is higher in the coastal lowlands than in the other regions, the coastlands produce almost 99% of Ecuador's agricultural exports and over half the food consumed in Ecuador.   Although the Andean highlands have almost half the national rural population, they produce a disproportionately small part of Ecuador's total agricultural output.

The most important response to the discrepancies between the distribution of population and the distribution of economic opportunities in Ecuador has been internal migration, both temporary and permanent.   For most of the twentieth century, it has been an

---

[11] Although some land is under cultivation in the Galapagos Islands and the agricultural area could be extended by irrigation, the author feels that the unique fauna and flora and remarkable topography of the islands justify their exclusive use as a national park for conservation, research and tourism, and hence preclude agricultural and industrial development.

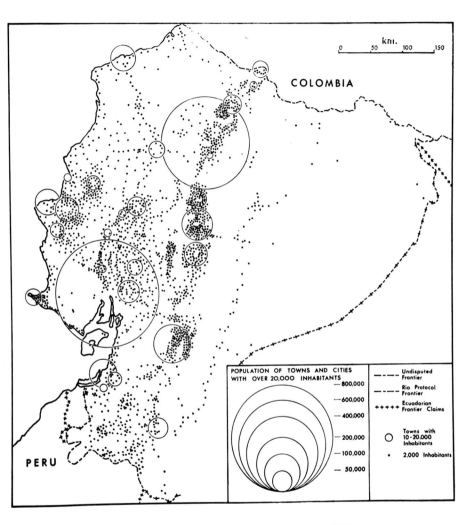

km.

0   50   100   150

COLOMBIA

PERU

POPULATION OF TOWNS AND CITIES WITH OVER 20,000 INHABITANTS	
— 800,000	
— 600,000	
— 400,000	
— 200,000	
— 100,000	
— 50,000	

– – – –	Undisputed Frontier
— ⋅ — ⋅ —	Rio Protocol Frontier
+ + + +	Ecuadorian Frontier Claims
◯	Towns with 10-20,000 Inhabitants
⋅	2,000 Inhabitants

FIGURE 4: POPULATION DISTRIBUTION IN 1974

established practice for many of the rural inhabitants of the Andean highlands to migrate seasonally to work in the plantations, estates and agricultural processing industries of the coastal lowlands (see Cisneros, 1959; Conforti, 1960, 31–2). This temporary migration has helped to alleviate the overpopulation of the Andean rural areas and the harvest labour shortage in the coastal lowlands. It has led to a limited flow of capital from the more developed coast to the less developed highlands, but it has generally failed to stimulate major development or innovation in the highlands. The temporary migration from the highlands to the rural areas and towns of the coastal lowlands has been accompanied by a substantial amount of permanent migration, particularly to the areas around Santo Domingo, Quevedo, Milagro and Machala. In addition, both temporary and permanent migration have been significant within the coastal lowlands, as people have moved from the semi-arid and drought-stricken areas of the Santa Elena peninsula and southern and central Manabí, to the more humid agricultural areas of northern Manabí and the Guayas basin. Both temporary and permanent migration have been significant from the Andean highlands to the nearest areas of the eastern lowlands, but this migration is much less important than the comparable movements to the coastal lowlands.

Over the last 30 years, the most important flow of both temporary and permanent migrants in Ecuador has been from rural areas and small towns to the larger towns and cities. This urbanization can be partially attributed to the low productivity of the agricultural sector (see UNECLA, 1961), the end of the coastal banana boom, the intense population pressure in many highland rural areas, and the failure to implement a real agrarian reform or to open up large areas of unused, potentially cultivable land in the coastal and eastern lowlands. Perhaps the most important factor, however, is that education, 'westernization' and increasing mobility have led to major changes in attitudes and values in the rural areas, particularly amongst the younger generation. In general, these have led to a growing dislike for the boredom, isolation and hard manual labour associated with rural farmwork, and a preference for change and variety rather than stability and security. Life in large towns and cities has proved particularly attractive because of the relatively easy access to shops, entertainments, schools and medical services, and the greater availability of electricity, piped water and motor transport.

30

The disparities between rural and urban areas in Ecuador and the widespread poverty that exists in the country, are well illustrated by the preliminary results of the 1974 national census (OCN, 1975), and particularly by the data on education and housing (Table 8). The rural areas of Ecuador have very poor levels of education and public service provision, reflecting the agglomeration of wealthier Ecuadorians in the urban areas, and the tendency of the Ecuadorian government to concentrate service provision in the towns. The strikingly different levels of service provision in urban and rural areas closely parallel the distribution of wealth and power in the country as a whole, perpetuating a situation of 'urban dominance' which has existed since the early Spanish colonial period, and which is continuously fuelled by the migration of rural dwellers seeking upward socio-economic mobility.

TABLE 8

RURAL-URBAN DISPARITIES IN EDUCATION AND HOUSING CONDITIONS IN 1974

Calculated from data in OCN (1975, 16–58).

	All Ecuador	Urban areas[1]	Rural areas[2]
Percentage of population over 9 who declare that they can read and write	75.1	90.4	63.5
Percentage of the population over 5 who have attended some			
Primary school	70.9	86.0	59.9
Secondary school	14.0	28.1	3.7
Higher Education	1.9	4.1	0.3
Percentage of occupied dwellings with			
Piped drinking-water supply in the dwelling ...	18.8	42.8	2.3
Electricity supply in the dwelling	40.6	82.4	12.0
A private toilet in the dwelling	18.4	40.3	3.3
Sanitation (sewerage or a cesspool)	40.4	83.3	11.0

1 'Urban' is defined in the Ecuadorian censuses as all settlements which are cantonal or provincial capitals. It includes a few settlements with less than 500 inhabitants.
2 'Rural' is defined in the Ecuadorian censuses as all settlements which are not cantonal or provincial capitals. Many of these settlements have over 1,000 inhabitants, and a few are decidedly urban in appearance (eg La Libertad in Guayas Province).

In the absence of more lucrative industrial employment, rural-urban migrants have generally found at least part-time employment in such tertiary occupations as domestic service, market and street trading, shoe-shining, and porterage. They usually earn only a meagre living, are often underemployed and may make only a minimal contribution to the national economy. However, many of these occupations have the advantage of being relatively easy to enter without much capital or training. The expansion of such tertiary occupations in Ecuador's towns and cities is essentially a reflection of urban economic stagnation rather than a proof of the Clark-Fisher thesis (Clark, 1940, 176–219; Fisher, 1945, 5–6) that growth in tertiary employment is a reflection of an increasingly affluent society.

Ecuador exhibits a rather unusual urban-size distribution with two separate primate cities, Guayaquil and Quito, whose respective populations in June 1974 were about 814,000 and 597,000 (OCN, 1974, 7 and 23). The third largest city, Cuenca, only had about 105,000 inhabitants in 1974 (OCN, 1974, 15). A further 17 towns, spread fairly evenly over the coastal lowlands and the Andean highlands, are each estimated to have a population of between 20,000 and 90,000.[12]

Recent studies of Ecuador's urban hierarchy by Dalmasso and Fillon (1970 and 1973) and by Deler (1975) have analysed the regional structure of Ecuador in terms of the different roles and spheres of influence of Quito and Guayaquil. For some functions, one or other city is clearly the dominant centre for the whole country, while in other cases Ecuador is effectively divided into separate hinterlands for Quito and Guayaquil. Quito is the dominant centre for government, higher education and tourism, while Guayaquil predominates in the import-export trade, wholesaling and banking. Data for internal migration, newspaper circulation, bus traffic and average daily road-traffic flows indicate two separate nodal regions. Guayaquil's hinterland covers almost all the coastal lowlands and much of the southern highlands and *Oriente*, while Quito's hinterland covers the central and northern highlands and *Oriente* and the northernmost part of the coastal lowlands. Ecuador's industrial census of 1965 showed that Quito had a slightly larger industrial and artisan labour force

---

[12] After Guayaquil, Quito and Cuenca, the next most important towns in Ecuador are Ambato (1974 population 77,000), Machala (68,000), Manta (64,000), Esmeraldas (60,000), Portoviejo (59,000), Riobamba (58,000) and Milagro (53,000). Source: OCN (1974).

than Guayaquil, but that the total value of industrial and artisan production in Guayaquil was considerably higher than in Quito (DGEC, 1969a, 5–7).

In Ecuador, there are two particularly striking spatial disparities in socio-economic conditions: the one between urban and rural areas, and particularly between the two metropoli and the remainder of the country; and the other between the more dynamic and commercialized coastal lowlands, and the more traditional and subsistence-oriented Andean highlands and eastern lowlands. Such disparities between more-developed 'core' areas and less-developed 'peripheral' areas are typical of most countries, and their existence helps to stimulate readjustments in the spatial structure of the economy through migration and capital flows. Hirschman (1958, 184) has pointed out that 'interregional inequality of growth is an inevitable concomitant and condition of growth itself', and it would appear that interregional inequalities generally tend to increase during the earlier stages of economic development (Williamson, 1965, 44). One of the most fundamental dilemmas faced by the governments of developing countries is whether to foster the most rapid national economic growth possible by allowing further concentration of development in the core areas, so increasing interregional inequalities, or to intervene in the location of economic activities and to reduce inequalities by diverting development from the core areas to the periphery. Increasing concentration of development in the core areas may lead to severe political and social tensions between the more privileged and less privileged regions, while 'an unprincipled redistribution of resources in favour of the periphery would significantly retard progress at the center, and consequently, for the country as a whole' (Friedmann, 1966, 13). The most suitable blend of concentration and dispersal policies must vary from country to country, depending upon the distribution of population and resources, the present pattern of inequalities, and the choice of suitable economic activities as growth sectors.

The response of the Ecuadorian government to the growing disparities in production and wealth between the different regions of the country, and between urban and rural areas, has so far been one of *laissez faire*. Private enterprise has generally been allowed to invest wherever and whenever it wishes, and government investment has tended to have a similar spatial distribution to that of private enterprise. Thus, there has been a great concentration of investment in and around

Quito and Guayaquil, encouraging the migration from the remainder of Ecuador towards these two cities. Most of Ecuador's 'resource frontiers', the large areas available for colonization, have been neglected, as have most of the densely-populated rural areas in the Andean highlands and coastal lowlands. The present distribution of government and private investment in Ecuador is closely related to the spatial distribution of wealth and power in the country, and is leading to the accentuation of this distribution by encouraging further investment in, and migration to, the most prosperous areas. Statistics on this topic are very scarce, and are usually presented on a provincial basis, thus masking most of the disparities between urban and rural areas. In spite of these problems, however, the disparities between Pichincha province, which includes Quito, Guayas province, which includes Guayaquil, and the remainder of the country are staggering (Table 9). In 1972, for example, the public sector income and expenditure in per capita terms for the province of Pichincha was 30 to 61 times greater than for the most backward provinces in the country, Bolívar, Napo, Morona-Santiago and Zamora-Chinchipe. In 1973, in per capita terms, the inhabitants of Pichincha and Guayas paid about 64 times more taxes and received about 92 times more government credit than the inhabitants of the eastern lowland provinces. Even though some of the facilities available in Pichincha and Guayas are used by the inhabitants of neighbouring provinces, so that taxes from other provinces may sometimes be paid in Pichincha and Guayas, and investments made and credits given in Pichincha and Guayas may benefit the inhabitants of other provinces, the elimination of these factors would probably not reduce disparities between provinces by more than 50%. If the cities of Quito and Guayaquil could be separated from the rest of Pichincha and Guayas, their advantages over the remainder of Ecuador would be even more striking. The national pattern of government income and expenditure is, in a *laissez faire* sense, a relatively fair one. The provinces which pay most get most and, on a more local scale, the people and neighbourhoods which pay most tend to get most. There is evidence that this pattern is becoming more marked through time, increasing the disparities between the two major cities and the remainder of the country. If this tendency continues, all of the areas of Ecuador outside the immediate localities of Quito and Guayaquil will gradually be converted into a vast 'national periphery', dependent upon the

34

TABLE 9

POPULATION, PUBLIC SECTOR ACCOUNTS, TAX REVENUE AND PUBLIC SECTOR BANK CREDITS, BY PROVINCES

	1974 population in thousands[1]	1972 public sector accounts in sucres per capita[2]		1973 tax revenue in sucres per capita[3]	1973 credit per capita extended by public sector banks (sucres)[4]
		Income	Expenditure		
HIGHLAND PROVINCES					
Carchi	120	253	407	47	753
Imbabura	218	253	363	89	245
Pichincha	981	6,123	6,910	1,123	953
Cotopaxi	236	178	288	51	167
Tungurahua ...	276	384	530	178	132
Bolívar	146	114	208	29	144
Chimborazo ...	306	218	329	70	203
Cañar	147	216	336	47	270
Azuay	366	563	779	332	203
Loja	343	213	346	50	196
COASTAL PROVINCES					
Esmeraldas ...	203	571	765	70	247
Manabí	809	321	434	80	763
Los Rios	384	219	305	23	378
Guayas	1,513	1,111	1,257	816	1,417
El Oro	260	614	757	95	875
EASTERN PROVINCES					
Napo	60	150	155	10	14
Pastaza	23	438	511	40	14
Morona–Santiago ...	50	104	114	7	14
Zamora–Chinchipe	35	123	230	17	11
GALAPAGOS	4	207	384	130	974
NATIONAL AVERAGE	—	1,460	1,613	418	721

1 Source: OCN (1974, 2).
2 Calculated from data in the Banco Central del Ecuador, Departamento de Política Fiscal. These accounts exclude the Central Government.
3 Source: MF (1974).
4 Calculated from data in the Banco Central del Ecuador, Departamento de Asuntos Monetarios, and the Super-intendencia de Bancos.
All per capita figures are related to the 1974 populations.

consumer and middleman demands emanating from the two metropoli, and upon the occasional hand-outs of the Ecuadorian government. The two major cities are gradually strengthening their positions as the centres of foreign influence, and as the points of articulation of foreign supply and demand in Ecuador. As a result, and with implicit government approval, Ecuador is being converted into the classic dependent economy described by Frank (1971), with national metropoli dominating the impoverished remainder of the country, and with the whole country being dependent upon the consumer demands, technological innovations, manufactured exports, cultural changes and 'aid', coming from the advanced western countries.

Race and class

Ecuador's internal inequalities in income and wealth, and especially the disparities which exist between different regions, and between urban and rural areas, all contribute to the country's relatively complex social structure. In order to understand this social structure fully, a knowledge of racial, cultural and linguistic variations within the country is essential. Ecuador's population is derived from three major ethnic groups: the Indians, who are descended from the indigenous population which lived in what is now Ecuador before the Spanish conquest in 1534; the 'whites', who are descended from the Spanish immigrants who came to Ecuador during the colonial period, and to a lesser extent, from European and North American immigrants who arrived in the nineteenth and twentieth centuries; and the negroes, who are mainly descended from slaves brought to the Andean countries by the Spaniards during the colonial period. In crude genetic terms, the Ecuadorian population is probably about 70% Indian, 25% Caucasian and 5% Negro. In reality, however, the situation is much more complex due to centuries of ethnic mixing. The Spanish colonial influence has led to the prevalence of a concept of 'white' superiority in Ecuador, with the members of the population having a high proportion of European ethnic origins generally occupying the highest social and economic strata and usually living in towns. The lower socio-economic strata and the rural population, generally have a higher proportion of Indian and/or negro origins. Because 'white' is a more desirable description to most Ecuadorians than 'Indian' or 'negro', upward social mobility and ethnic mixture has generally led to the absorption of most ethnically-mixed groups into the 'white' category. Thus, 'white' is no longer equivalent to Caucasian, but rather reflects any ethnic, cultural and linguistic combination which is not clearly Indian or negro.

The surviving Indian element in Ecuador makes up only about 20% of the national population. Almost all of the Indians speak Indian languages, but most also have a reasonable knowledge of Spanish. Since the Spanish conquest, the Indians have been the victims of discrimination and exploitation (eg Burgos, 1970; Cueva, 1972; Villavicencio R, 1973) by the westernized, Spanish-speaking inhabitants who today make up the majority of Ecuador's population. Most of the Indians are concentrated in the Andean highlands as Quechua-speaking farmers and estate workers, while a few more primitive groups of farmers, hunters and gatherers are found in the eastern lowlands and the northern coastlands. The Indians generally live away from the non-Indian population and form Ecuador's lowest social and economic stratum. The principal concentrations of Indians in Ecuador are in the higher-altitude rural areas of the pro-vinces of Imbabura, Cotopaxi, Tungurahua, Bolívar, Chimborazo and Cañar. Over the last 400 years, the proportion of Indians in the national population has gradually declined due to the immigration of non-Indian peoples, racial interbreeding, the high mortality of the Indian population and the absorption of those Indians who adopt the Spanish language and western dress into the majority 'white'[13] culture. By these means alone, however, it will take several more centuries for the 'Indian problem' to disappear. In the meantime, the Indian population is a potentially valuable human resource which at present is almost wasted, playing only a small part in the Ecuadorian economy and often having little real concept of nationality (see Bonifaz, 1975, 81–2).

---

13 Following colloquial Ecuadorian terminology, 'white' refers to all Ecuadorians who are not usually known as Indians or negroes. It includes *mestizos*, *cholos* and others who are of mixed race or of Indian origin, but have adopted dress, language and customs of European origin. Good summaries of the complexities of race and class in Ecuador are available in Weinstock (1970, 157–61) and Whitten (1974, 174–201).

Over more than four centuries, the Indian population has been progressively 'marginalized', so that they are now concentrated in the most backward and remote areas of the country and in the most stagnant sectors of the economy. Most of the areas with a dense Indian population have a severe shortage of potentially cultivable land, as well as problems of soil erosion and lack of irrigation water. The majority of the Indian population are poor and malnourished, and many are chronic alcoholics. Their response to their position at the bottom of the Ecuadorian socio-economic hierarchy has generally been one of passive submission. For centuries, the Indians have been exploited by 'white' landowners, commercial intermediaries, priests and officials, and the most frequent response to programmes of government assistance is one of apathetic rejection. The Indian population is generally hard-working, and can show remarkable entrepreneurial skill (see Preston, 1963), but the legacy of exploitation means that a programme to improve their socio-economic situation must involve a large-scale redistribution of land and commercial opportunities and requires a continuous effort in the fields of education, community development and technical assistance, for at least three decades. No such commitment has ever been made by the Ecuadorian government. The attempts at agrarian reform since the law of 1964 have done no more for most of the Indian population than to convert them from serfs to impoverished small farmers or landless labourers (see Peñaherrera and Costales, 1971). A great deal has been written about the International Labour Office's Andean Programme to improve the living standards of the highland Indians (eg D'Ugard, 1966; Rens, 1965; MAE, 1972), but the results of this programme have been negligible in relation to the size of the 'Indian problem'. The Andean Programme was established as a joint venture by various international organizations under the leadership of the International Labour Office, initially working in Ecuador, Peru and Bolivia. In Ecuador, the Programme adopted the title 'Andean Mission', was gradually transferred from the international organizations to the Ecuadorian government between 1959 and 1964, and was finally incorporated into the Ministry of Agriculture's Rural Development Division in 1973. It began as a small, enthusiastic and moderately effective local programme in Chimborazo province, evolved into a bureaucratic national government organization based in Quito and working in six different provinces, and eventually lost its identity altogether as a special

38

programme to help rural Indian groups. The Andean Mission never received sufficient government resources to have a great effect and many of the resources that it did receive were dissipated in bureaucracy, operational inefficiency and impractical projects. It facilitated the building of a substantial number of local roads and schools and introduced some new crops and handicrafts to rural areas, but it failed to effect any real change in the socio-economic status of the Indian (see Marroquin, 1972, 178–80). Like agrarian reform, the Andean Mission was thrust upon Ecuador by the pressure of international organizations and foreign-aid 'donors' (see ILO, 1953, 30–8; Johnston, 1970, 258–9). Also like agrarian reform, it was doomed to failure from the start through the lack of real government support, continuing as a mere charade to impress aid 'donors' and to satisfy local pressure groups (see Hurtado and Herudek, 1974, 95–8).

Ecuadorian intellectuals have shown much less interest in their indigenous origins than their counterparts in Mexico or Bolivia, and *indigenismo* is a poorly-developed movement in Ecuador. The Ecuadorian upper classes tend to view the Indian population as an obstacle to progress, and the theory that the Indians are genetically inferior is frequently advanced (*eg* Bonifaz, 1975, 22–36). A deep-rooted concern to right the wrongs inflicted upon the Indian population is only rarely found amongst upper-class Ecuadorians and there is a general resistance to the principle of ethno-cultural equality in a truly plural society. When it has not oppressed the Indian, 'white' society has tended to expect the Indian to improve himself by learning 'white' customs, so that Indian society has often been polarized into the 'progressives' who abandon their Indian customs and become 'whites', and the 'die-hards', who retreat into retrogressive isolationism.

The 'negro problem' in Ecuador is smaller and less widely recognized than the 'Indian problem', but it is still very significant. Ecuador's negro and mulatto population is concentrated in the northwest of the country, and particularly in the province of Esmeraldas. The majority of the negroes are small-scale rural farmers, agricultural labourers and forestry workers, but an increasing number are settling in the slum neighbourhoods of the town of Esmeraldas and the cities of Guayaquil and Quito, taking up occupations as construction labourers, petty traders and domestic servants. If they adopt 'white' dress and customs, and if they manage to accumulate a little wealth, Indians can become 'white' because the physical differences between

39

Indians and 'whites' are relatively insignificant. For negroes, however, absorption into the 'white' population is impossible because of the marked physical differences between negroes and 'whites'. The Ecuadorian negro is generally conceived by members of the 'white' population to be poor, lazy and stupid (see Whitten, 1974, 174–201), and he is the victim of many forms of discrimination and prejudice. Even in the province of Esmeraldas, where the majority of the population are negroes, the leading landowners, merchants and officials are almost univerally 'white'. Though Ecuador has not yet seen many assertions of 'Black Power', the negroes are likely to become increasingly resentful of their inferior socio-economic standing, and of the neglect of the areas where they are numerically predominant. As a result, racial conflict may be difficult to avoid in the future.

Ecuador has a relatively complex and rigid class structure based on differences in property, income, education, culture and race. Using social, cultural and economic data, Torres Caicedo (1960, 28) has divided Ecuador's population into three basic social classes as follows: upper class 1.2%; middle class 20.7%; and lower class 78.1%. This division emphasizes the strongly pyramidal character of Ecuador's class structure and the high concentration of wealth and power in a very small upper class.

Ecuador's middle class of 'white-collar workers' and professionals is gradually increasing in size, but has achieved little social or economic identity and possesses less political power than the upper class or foreign-interest groups (see Hurtado, 1969, 177; König, 1972, 115–46). The middle class has, so far, contributed relatively little to social or economic change beyond a continual expansion of government power and bureaucracy. This failure can be attributed to three major factors: the oligopolistic control of foreign and Ecuadorian elites over many sectors of the Ecuadorian economy; the tendency for middle-class groups in Ecuador to copy blindly the attitudes, values and consumption habits of national and foreign elites; and the problems of working within a system where 'creative forces are paralyzed by almost permanently-rigid bureaucratic structures, and by the insecurity of employment resulting from political instability' (König, 1972, 122).

Torres Caicedo's enormous 'lower class' is little more than an agglomeration of residual groups once one has identified an upper class and a middle class. It has little identity, and even less solidarity.

Effectively, the lower class is divided between rural groups and urban groups, and each of these categories is further subdivided by region, by ownership or lack of ownership of property, and by type of employment.

The rural lower-class population can be divided into three principal groups: firstly, the moderately well-off small-to-medium scale farmers who do not usually seek work outside their own properties, and who often employ wage labourers; secondly, the impoverished very small-scale farmers (*minifundistas*) who eke out a meagre living on their plots and usually seek outside work locally or as temporary migrants, earning money as farm labourers, urban construction workers, petty traders and artisans; and thirdly, the landless rural farm workers who depend for their living on employment opportunities offered by medium- and large-scale farmers. The first group, the moderately well-off small-to-medium scale farmers, are mainly found in the coastal and eastern lowlands. The second group, the *minifundistas*, are mainly found in the Andean highlands. The third group, the landless rural workers, are found throughout the populated rural areas of Ecuador, but are especially important in the main export crop-producing zone which stretches from Santo Domingo in the north through to Machala in the south, forming a relatively narrow strip, 10 to 40 kilometres wide, along the western fringe of the Andes. The rural lower-class groups are further divided between 'whites', Indians and negroes, with the Indians and negroes usually occupying the lowest niches in the socio-economic hierarchy, and being concentrated in the least productive and most impoverished agricultural areas.

The urban lower-class population is, if anything, even more divided than the rural lower class. Ethno-cultural divisions between 'whites', Indians and negroes are much less important than in rural areas because of the numerical insignificance of Indians and negroes in most urban areas in Ecuador. However, there is an intense subdivision of occupations, with each occupation and scale of operation having different working conditions. The principal division is between the 'blue-collar' unionized factory workers, who possess considerable group solidarity and have achieved moderate wages, reasonable job security and eligibility for social security, and the overwhelming mass of the urban poor who are self-employed, or employed individually in houses or small workshops, and who tend

41

to have lower wages and little job security, and are often not eligible for social security. The 'blue-collar' unionized factory workers (usually described as modern sector or formal sector workers) form a 'lower-class elite', but are numerically unimportant on a national scale. This 'proletariat' makes up under 5% of the urban economically-active population in Ecuador (OCN, 1975, 30). Much more important is the 'subproletariat' (see Cueva, 1973, 88–90) or 'protoproletariat' (see McGee, 1974), who make up over 75% of the urban economically-active population (OCN, 1975, 30). This diverse group of small-scale artisans, traders, transporters and repairers, and of workers in personal and domestic service, can be crudely described as the 'informal sector' or 'traditional sector'. This sector generally lacks effective trade union organization, has little job security, receives little assistance from government, and is inadequately recorded in government statistics. Socially, the 'subproletariat' is deeply divided and lacks any effective group solidarity.

The division of lower-class interests in Ecuador is accentuated by the division of the trade union movement into three ideologically contrasting groups: CEDOC,[14] a federation of trade unions with radical, Christian democrat leanings; CTE,[15] a federation of trade unions with Moscow-oriented communist sympathies; and CEOSL,[16] a federation of trade unions with strong anti-communist feelings which has received considerable backing from the United States' trade union organizations, and from the United States' government (see Hurtado and Herudek, 1974, 69–81). In 1973, it is estimated that CTE-federated 800 union groups with a total of 40,000 members, CEDOC-federated 750 union groups with 37,500 members and CEOSL-federated 600 union groups with 32,500 members. In addition to this, there were some 2,200 independent union groups with about 110,000 members, including the most powerful union of all, the National Federation of Professional Drivers (Hurtado and Herudek, 1974, 89). The intense subdivision of the trade union movement, with one-half of the union members being divided between three opposing federations, and the other half being organized in a multiplicity of independent unions, has impeded the development of any form of lower-class solidarity in Ecuador. It should also be

---

14 *Central Ecuatoriana de Organizaciones Clasistas.*
15 *Confederación de Trabajadores del Ecuador.*
16 *Confederación Ecuatoriana de Organizaciones Sindicales Libres.*

remembered that less than 12% of the economically-active population of Ecuador belong to a union group, and that many of these groups are totally ineffective. Many trade union leaders have used their positions for personal enrichment (see *eg* Hurtado and Herudek, 1974, 81–2), and some have converted themselves into successful managers, speculators, or populist politicians. The trade union movement has failed to achieve any great advances for the Ecuadorian lower class. Indeed, through its own subdivision and internal corruption, it has facilitated an elite strategy of 'divide and rule'.

CHAPTER III

Political Changes Since 1948

FOR ECUADOR, the twentieth century has been a succession of economic booms and depressions, each boom period being one of relative political stability, and each depression period being one of great instability. The first major boom occurred between 1905 and 1920, and was based upon large-scale cocoa exports at a time of high prices and rapidly-expanding world demand. The boom ended with a gradual fall in world prices during the 1920s, and with the progressive infestation of Ecuador's plantations by *Monilla* and Witchbroom diseases. The combination of the collapse of cocoa exports in the 1920s and the world depression which began in 1929 led Ecuador into a period of economic stagnation and severe political instability. Between the beginning of 1931 and the end of 1948, Ecuador had 21 different Presidents, two of them, José María Velasco Ibarra and Carlos Arroyo del Río, holding two separate Presidential terms (Maier, 1969b, 32–3). During this period, Ecuador was the most politically unstable of the Latin American republics (USDOS, 1966, 86), the country's grave instability reflecting economic depression and uncertainty, and the inability of any single political party or dictatorial leader to maintain a hold on power.

The political context

Ecuadorian politics have four particularly distinctive features: a very limited electoral franchise; a seemingly never-ending dispute about which of many possible constitutions should be used; an intense subdivision of the major political parties; and a strong tendency for political parties to be focussed around dominant individuals and to subdivide whenever there are major differences of opinion between political leaders.

Perhaps the strongest indication that Ecuador is ruled by her minority upper and middle classes, and not by popular votes in a truly democratic system, is the system of franchise which exists in the country. Only literate citizens aged 18 or over, and possessing an identity card, can be registered to vote in elections, and only registered voters can actually vote. Though registered voters are expected by law to vote, many do not. The result is that:

> 'in elections since 1948 the percentage of the population casting a vote has never reached 20%, and on occasion has dropped beneath 10%. With mass electoral participation so limited, there is consequently less direct pressure on the parties to make good their promises . . . So long as illiterates are denied the vote, party leaders will find it easy to maintain a basic commitment to the *status quo* rather than to work for the adoption of progressive reforms' (Martz, 1972, 109).

The limitation of the franchise to literate, documented, registered citizens, means that only about half Ecuador's adult population are entitled to vote, and that the majority of the lower class is excluded from electoral participation. In particular, the rural vote is markedly reduced by this limitation, and the overwhelming majority of the Indian and negro populations are excluded from formal politics. The Ecuadorian upper and middle classes clearly fear the potential electoral weight of numbers of the lower class and use the criteria of literacy, documentation and registration to prevent this weight of numbers from having any real effect. The limitation of franchise also reflects the paternalistic attitudes of many well-off Ecuadorians, who consider peasants, Indians, illiterates and other underprivileged groups as no more significant than children. Indeed, a common paternalistic mode of address used by 'white' officials towards adult Indians is *mi hijo* (my son), or even *mi niñito* (my little child).

The failure of the Ecuadorian government to introduce universal adult suffrage is a strong indication of the continuity of elite domination of Ecuadorian politics. Indeed, the last attempt to change the suffrage laws was actually intended to reduce the size of the electorate still further (Maier, 1969b, 49). If one uses the terms 'left-wing', 'politically central' and 'right-wing', in the way that they are used in Europe, or even in North America, then it is realistic to state that Ecuador has never had a 'left-wing' government. Ecuador's governments have oscillated between the political centre and the political right, always avoiding a real swing to the left which would imply fundamental changes in the distribution of wealth and power in the country.

The issue of the limited franchise in Ecuador has attracted much less political controversy than the issue of Presidential power *vis-à-vis* the Congress. This latter issue has been disputed for most of Ecuador's history, and is still far from settled. Sixteen different constitutions have been operative since Ecuador's independence (see Maier, 1969b, 31; Martz, 1972, 78–9). Currently, the operative constitution is that of 1946, which has been in force since 1970, when the 1967 constitution was annulled. The frequency of constitutional changes, combined with the frequency of Presidential changes, reflects Ecuador's basic political instability. Perhaps the best summary of this instability and of its relationship to right-wing control of Ecuadorian political processes, is given by Maier (1969b, 21–2) in an historical survey of Ecuadorian politics since independence:

'A different government every 1.7 years and a different constitution every 8.5 years may lead one to the conclusion that Ecuador's political system is highly unstable. If a system's instability is measured by phenomena such as numbers of *coups d'état*, the use of violence and terror as political instruments, and insecurity of tenure for constitutionally established governments, then Ecuador certainly fits the description. Yet these phenomena so frequent in the country's political history have had little if any effect on the structure of power relationships. The socio-economic elite of the Sierra and the Costa have continued to rule the country, either directly or by holding key government positions . . . Ecuador is managed by a "divided elite" whose members fight over control of the government at election time. On economic and social questions, however, they present a united front. To maintain the most sacred institutions of the *status quo*, they make certain that their political differences do not endanger it'.

In the nineteenth century, Ecuador had only two basic political parties, the Conservative Party, founded in 1869, and the Liberal Party,[17] founded in 1878. In the 1920s, two very small parties were established on the political left, the Socialist Party, founded in 1926, and the Communist Party, founded in 1927 (Maier, 1969b, 67). These four parties were the basis of Ecuadorian politics until the early 1940s, when a process of intense political subdivision began.

[17] The Liberal Party is officially called the Radical-Liberal Party, though it has not shown any major element of radicalism since 1920.

46

This subdivision has continued through to the present day, and there are now at least 20 different political parties, the actual number of parties varying from month to month as new ones are founded and some old ones lapse. About half of the present parties are subdivisions of the four older ones, whilst the others are newer parties, most of them focussed around the political philosophies of their founder-leaders. The key to an understanding of Ecuador's numerous and intensely subdivided political parties is 'personalism', the cult of the individual. The egotism and quarrelsome nature of most of the major political leaders has meant that they are unwilling to tolerate competition for leadership within their own parties. Successful aspirants to party leadership tend to expel their rivals, while unsuccessful aspirants tend to found their own parties. Ideological clashes within particular parties tend to lead to the division of the parties into smaller, more ideologically coherent groups. The only control on this continual subdivision of parties seems to be the fact that many of the smaller parties eventually die out because of shortage of funds or lack of enthusiasm on the part of their leaders. Most of the political parties have little or no activity outside election periods, and Ecuadorian political activity is extremely ephemeral. The prevalence of personalism in Ecuadorian politics reflects the traditional selfishness and lack of ideology of the Ecuadorian elites, and also the intense socio-economic subdivisions which beset the Ecuadorian upper class. These characteristics of the political process can be attributed to Ecuador's relative lack of democratic political maturity, to the upper-class control of politics, and to the limited electoral franchise, factors which impede the development of genuine mass movements. Most Presidential candidates run with the support of several different political parties, so that elections are essentially contests between rival coalitions. These coalitions, however, usually dissolve immediately after each election, and the alliances at later elections often bear little or no resemblance to those at earlier elections. In each election, a substantial number of political parties, and particularly of left-wing parties, are prohibited from campaigning, or are simply 'unrecognized by the government', so that the political process has few stable elements beyond the personalities of key party leaders.[18]

18 Descriptions of the main political parties in contemporary Ecuador are given by Maier (1969b, 35–47), Martz (108–45) and the Ecuadorian magazine *Nueva* (No 21, julio 1975, 20–39).

The subdivision and instability of Ecuador's political parties, and the key role played by individual politicians in national politics, have both encouraged the country's basic political instability. The concentration of high-level political activity amongst the country's socio-economic elites, has meant that many leading politicians are inter-related, and that several of Ecuador's Presidents have been close relatives of ex-Presidents. Personalistic politics are intimately related to favouritism and nepotism, and all of these deplorable tendencies are carried over from politics into public administration and business. The continual uncertainty faced by politicians and civil servants in such a politically unstable country often leads to a 'get-rich-quick' attitude at all levels of government with a deplorable degree of corruption, particularly at the lower levels of administration. Ties of influence and friendship have frequently caused the appointment of untrained and incapable administrators, and some politicians and administrators assume office more concerned to build a personal fortune and to improve the status of their family and friends than to implement any serious programme of development or reform. Administrative corruption in Ecuador has altered the results of elections (*eg* Cueva, 1973, 48–53), toppled governments (*eg* Agee, 206–95), provoked military *coup d'états*, and entrenched multinational companies in Ecuadorian markets (*eg* Galarza, 1974, 135–301; Paredes, 1970, 139–206; Vera Arrata, 1972). Corruption is part of the national socio-political system, and must be included in any explanation of why leaders may betray their followers, why governments may fail to keep their promises, and why official actions may be almost unrelated to official words. Corruption, personalism and bureaucratic inefficiency, are all major forces of stability in Ecuador, frustrating pressures for change and helping to maintain the existing distribution of wealth and power. Perhaps the most depressing feature of administrative corruption is the part played by foreign companies and governments in increasing the level of corruption and maladministration in Ecuadorian society as a means to promote their own interests. Both bribery and coercion by foreign-interest groups are symptomatic of Ecuador's external dependency.

In considering the context of Ecuadorian politics, it would be unfair to omit another symptom of Ecuador's foreign dependence, the prevalence of 'developmentalism' (*desarrollismo*) amongst many of its politicians and civil servants. Developmentalism, in its crudest sense, is the desire to imitate the more developed, western countries, pressing Ecuador as rapidly as possible towards the adoption of sophisticated technology, modern industry, mass production and luxury consumption. It leads towards a high dependence upon imported goods, services and technical expertise, a national inferiority complex *vis-à-vis* the more 'modern' countries of North America and Western Europe, and the rapid acquisition of western attitudes, values and tastes. The application of developmentalist ideas tends to stimulate economic growth, but to accentuate foreign dependence. It intensifies social and economic dualism, separating the country into modern, westernized enclaves, and backward, traditional peripheries. Naturally, it tends to widen socio-economic inequalities, and to stimulate the more blatant forms of materialism, producing a revolution of rising, but unsatisfiable, expectations. Developmentalism has been a significant doctrine in Ecuador since the late 1940s, and is probably only just passing its peak as the euphoria of the post-1972 'oil boom' begins to fade.

Political change

The elections of 1948, won by the Liberal Party's candidate Galo Plaza Lasso, the son of an ex-President, ushered in twelve years of relative political stability and an economic boom period based on banana exports. Three successive Presidents completed their four-year terms and four successive direct popular Presidential elections determined who should occupy the Presidency (Table 10). The uniqueness of this period in Ecuadorian history is reflected by the fact that, since Ecuador's independence in 1830, there have only been seven elections when the President was constitutionally and democratically 'elected in a more or less free atmosphere, *ie*, when a candidate was not imposed on the electorate or when wholesale fraud in the manipulation of votes did not occur' (Maier, 1971, 483).[19] These

[19] Maier considers that eight such elections took place in a more or less free atmosphere, but, from the evidence given by Cueva (1973, 50–3) on the 1940 election, this election must surely be discounted, leaving the seven listed above.

49

seven free elections took place in 1875, 1934, 1948, 1952, 1956, 1960 and 1968; four of them in the period 1948–1960. Relative democracy is a rare phenomenon in Ecuador, and the 1948 to 1960 period is the most significant period of constitutional, democratic rule in the country's history. Of course, the stable Presidential succession between 1948 and 1960 does not necessarily indicate total political stability. Ministerial changes were much more frequent than Presidential changes and were inevitably accompanied by substantial changes in government personnel. In addition, there were occasional outbreaks of political unrest, the most famous one being the Guayaquil riots in 1959, which were viciously put down by the government with many rioters being killed or wounded (Cueva, 1973, 68).

TABLE 10

PRESIDENTS OF ECUADOR, 1948–1976

Principal source: Maier (1969b, 32–3).

Chief Executive	From	To
Galo Plaza Lasso	1 Sept 1948	31 Aug 1952
José María Velasco Ibarra	1 Sept 1952	31 Aug 1956
Camilo Ponce Enríquez	1 Sept 1956	31 Aug 1960
José María Velasco Ibarra ...	1 Sept 1960	9 Nov 1961
Carlos Julio Arosemena	9 Nov 1961	11 July 1963
Military Junta	11 July 1963	29 Mar 1966
Clemente Yerovi Indaburo ...	30 Mar 1966	15 Nov 1966
Otto Arosemena Gómez	16 Nov 1966	31 Aug 1968
José María Velasco Ibarra ...	1 Sept 1968	15 Feb 1972
Guillermo Rodríguez Lara ...	15 Feb 1972	11 Jan 1976
Military Junta	11 Jan 1976	—

Galo Plaza's Presidency marked the large-scale introduction of developmentalism to Ecuador. Plaza, a leading *hacienda* owner, and a personal friend of Nelson Rockefeller, was concerned to bring the benefits of modernity to Ecuador, welcoming foreign investment, promoting modern technology, and encouraging the streamlining of government and the introduction of modern management and planning techniques (see Plaza, 1955, 20–43). Plaza's Presidency paralleled the ascendancy of the banana as the basis of Ecuador's economy, and Plaza subsequently jointly wrote a book praising the leading United States' banana company (May and Plaza, 1958). It was a period of prosperity for the merchant elites and the growing middle class, and it marked a considerable strengthening of foreign dependence, particularly in the economic, technological and cultural fields.

The successor to Plaza, Dr José María Velasco Ibarra, had already had two uncompleted Presidential terms, one in the 1930s, when he had been elected to power, and one in the 1940s, when he had assumed power some years after losing the 1940 elections through an electoral fraud (see Cueva, 1973, 50–3). Velasco, a prolific writer and incorrigible demagogue, has dominated Ecuadorian political life since the 1930s, and is the Ecuadorian political figure who is most worthy of international fame. His Presidential term from 1952 to 1956 was the third of five separate Presidential terms, each of them, with the possible exception of the 'postponed' term in the 1940s, resulting directly from an electoral victory. Velasco has never behaved as a 'strong man', autocratically dominating his government and armed forces, and holding power with an iron fist. Instead, he has relied upon electoral victories to give him power, and has only managed to complete one of his five Presidential terms.

Velasco was born in 1893 to a Conservative family, and was educated as a lawyer. His politics have always lacked ideology, and he has generally steered clear of the traditional political parties. Throughout his career, Velasco has been pitifully thin (one of his nicknames is 'The Skeleton'), childless, and relatively poor. He has often been manipulated by corrupt politicians and his regimes have been characterized by administrative inefficiency and corruption, unpredictable shifts of policy, financial instability and devaluation, and the growing unpopularity of the government. Velasco has been the brunt of almost every form of ridicule, has fought many battles with a recalcitrant Congress, and has been forced out of power four times by mounting popular discontent and military coups. His commonest nickname is 'the old madman' (*el viejo loco*), and, except at election time, no-one except his immediate lieutenants seems to have a good word for him. Though his language is strongly nationalist and he was responsible for Ecuador's rejection of the Rio Protocol, he has generally failed to counter Ecuador's growing foreign dependency and has usually followed a middle-of-the-road political line, favouring foreign investment in Ecuador. He has, however, tended

51

to ridicule technocrats and planners, and has favoured a more personalistic and paternalistic style of government decision making. During his Presidencies, he has travelled widely over the country, listening to local petitions and promising government action like a Presidential Santa Claus. His regimes have generally been characterized by a high concentration on public works, though the majority of these works have never been completed because of financial problems or Velasco's eventual overthrow. When he has not been President, much of Velasco's time has been spent in exile, generally in Buenos Aires. At the time of the writing of this monograph in 1976, and at the ripe old age of 83, Velasco is waiting in Buenos Aires for his 'sixth coming', and his *Velasquista* party machine in Ecuador is still preparing for his triumphant return.

To explain Velasco's incredible success in Ecuadorian politics, undoubtedly winning four democratic, constitutional popular elections, probably winning a fifth, and holding power for a total of almost 13 years, one can do no better than to read Cueva's (1973) excellent analysis. Cueva stresses Velasco's qualities as an orator, his ability to relate to the common man and to denounce the rich and powerful, his Saint-like honesty, poverty and personal austerity, and his ideological flexibility, allowing him to appeal to widely different groups. He also stresses the Ecuadorian population's lack of political maturity, the weakness and subdivision of the traditional political parties, and the tendency for political pressure to build up before an election and virtually to disappear after the election until a time of crisis, or the next election. Most important of all, however, in Cueva's analysis, is the fact that Velasco has been backed by many members of the upper and middle classes. This backing has been given because Velasco offers a better opportunity than any other potential President to reap the spoils of power, and because his brand of non-ideological populism has been used to avoid the development of a genuine leftist political regime with the widespread support of the lower class. Thus, a swing to the left in Ecuador has been avoided because most potential left-wing votes have been mopped up by the politically middle-of-the-road *Velasquistas*.

Velaso's 1952–1956 Presidency was perhaps his most successful ever. Holding power as banana exports continued to rise, he lasted his full Presidential term, initiating grandiose public works programmes and bankrupting the Treasury (see Martz, 1972, 71–2). As

52

the outgoing President, Velasco was unable to run in the 1956 election, which was won by a right-wing candidate, Camilo Ponce Enríquez, effectively representing the Conservative Party. Ponce's Presidency continued the *desarrollista* political line initiated by Plaza, but was more troubled than either of the two preceding Presidents' terms because of economic problems and the rumblings of left-wing political discontent which culminated in the bloody Guayaquil riots of 1959. The 1960 elections were overwhelmingly won by Velasco, who defeated three other candidates, including Galo Plaza.

Velasco's fourth Presidency, which followed the 1960 elections, was short and unsuccessful. He inherited serious economic problems, alienated most of the armed forces, quarrelled with his Vice-President, Carlos Julio Arosemena Monroy, and fell foul of all political parties in trying to define a national foreign policy in a period of left-wing hope and right-wing reaction following the Communist take-over in Cuba. 1961 marked the first intimations of the end of the banana export boom. Though bananas continued as the main export until they were replaced by oil in the second half of 1972, the 1961–1971 period in Ecuador was marked by frequent balance-of-payments crises and great economic uncertainty (see Zuvekas, 1968). The root of these problems was the resurgence of the Central American banana producers on the world market, the inelasticity of world demand for bananas, the impact of Panama and Sigatoka diseases on Ecuadorian banana production and the failure of Ecuadorian banana producers to switch rapidly from their traditional Gros Michel variety to the newer hybrid Cavendish variety (see Preston, 1965; Valles, 1968). The Ecuadorian economy was once more the victim of its own dependence upon fickle international markets and multi-national companies. Throughout the 1960s, Ecuador produced too many bananas, sold too few and obtained low prices for her product. 1961 was a year of rapid inflation and a serious economic crisis provoked by a sharp fall in banana and coffee exports (Cueva, 1973, 69–70). Velasco's attempts to save the economy through widespread tax increases led to a succession of strikes, protests and riots, culminating in an intervention by the armed forces, who deposed Velasco and installed Arosemena Monroy as provisional President.

Arosemena Monroy came from one of the wealthiest Guayaquil merchant and industrialist families, and hence was politically acceptable to most of the Ecuadorian right wing. At the same time, he had connexions with left-wing intellectuals and flirted with the political left. Arosemena Monroy's presidential policies generally placed him in, or to the right of, the political centre, but he was the victim of a smear campaign. This campaign depicted Arosemena's harmless flirtations with the left as steps towards Communism, and condemned Arosemena's drunkenness, swearing and anti-American outbursts. There can be little doubt that the campaign was orchestrated by right-wing and American political interests (see Agee, 1975, 206–95; Roucek, 1965). It led to the overthrow of Arosemena Monroy by the armed forces and the imposition of an authoritarian, right-wing Military Junta.

The four-man Military Junta which took power in 1963 was, if anything, even more developmentalist than Plaza or Ponce's regimes. It attempted to eliminate administrative corruption and inefficiency, to clamp down on left-wing sympathisers and to impose fundamental reforms, the most important being the Agrarian Reform Law of 1964. After a few months of power, however, it was already clear that the Military Junta had underestimated the problems of eliminating corruption and inefficiency, and that many of their policies were paralysed by political opposition or by the country's economic problems. The Military Junta greatly underestimated the difficulties of achieving real reforms in Ecuador and became increasingly unpopular because of its dictatorial attitudes. The leaders within the regime quarrelled, the regime became increasingly repressive, and eventually the Junta resigned in 1966 after widespread anti-government strikes and riots.

The 1963–1966 Military Junta was succeeded by two rather short-lived Presidents, Clemente Yerovi Indaburo, a middle-of-the-road provisional President who ruled until a constituent assembly could be convened, and then Otto Arosemena Gómez, who was elected as provisional President by the constituent assembly for the period before the expected Presidential election. Yerovi achieved little in his Presidency beyond establishing a climate of relative stability. Arosemena Gómez, a cousin of Arosemena Monroy, however, made a rather more forceful showing, following an independent right-wing line with similar economic and social policies to those of Plaza and Ponce. The 1968 elections were narrowly won by Velasco, who beat four other candidates, including Camilo Ponce (see Maier, 1969b; Wright, 1970).

Velasco's fifth Presidential term, which began in 1968, was marked by economic problems, but also by the expectation of the 'oil bonanza', due to begin before the end of the Presidential term with the completion of the 503-kilometre Trans-Andean pipeline connecting the Texaco-Gulf fields in the north-east to the Pacific near Esmeraldas. The whole of Velasco's fifth Presidency was enlivened by the complex negotiations with Texaco-Gulf and the other companies prospecting for oil and gas in different parts of Ecuador. Problems of administrative corruption were probably more severe than in any regime since 1948, and the ageing Velasco was at his most erratic and irascible. Velasco soon quarrelled with the Congress, and in June 1970 he annulled the 1967 constitution, dissolved Congress, and assumed dictatorial powers with the support of the armed forces. The patience of the armed forces in not taking power themselves can only be explained by their reluctance to repeat the painful experience of 1963–1966. Velasco's assumption of dictatorial powers was soon followed by a drastic 28% devaluation of the national currency, the sucre, from around 18 to the US dollar to 25 to the US dollar. Banana, cocoa and coffee sales failed to improve and the government was forced to borrow heavily abroad, mortgaging its future oil revenues. Velasco survived an abortive coup by dissident military officers led by General Luis Jacome Chávez in April 1971, but was eventually overthrown and sent into exile by the armed forces in February 1972, when a military government was established under the leadership of General Guillermo Rodríguez Lara.

In explaining the 1972 military coup, two factors are particularly significant. First, as 1972 was the year when oil exports began, the new government only had to last a few months before the beginning of the long-awaited 'oil bonanza'. Second, 1972 was the year when elections were due, and the overthrow of Velasco was certainly intended to avoid a national election. The concern of the armed forces to avoid an election was really based on their fear of one potential candidate, the Guayaquil politician Asaad Bucaram, leader of the anti-establishment CFP[20] political party. Since 1960, through successfully holding office as Mayor of Guayaquil, and then as Prefect of Guayas province, Bucaram had built himself a considerable power base in Guayas and the neighbouring coastal provinces. In political

---

[20] *Concentración de Fuerzas Populares*, literally Concentration of Popular Forces.

philosophy he is rather similar to Velasco, avoiding any definable political ideology, making frequent nationalistic statements, appealing to the masses, denouncing the oligarchy and remaining studiously imprecise on most major policy issues (see *Nueva*, No 20, June 1975, 50–61). Bucaram has the potential to convert himself into a second Velasco, mobilizing immense electoral support for his personalistic brand of populism. He has been surrounded by a similar group of get-rich-quick politicians to those who have always surrounded Velasco, but his style is rather more repressive and vicious than Velasco's. A Bucaram-led CFP government in Ecuador might take the country to the left of the political centre for the first time, but it is probably more likely to oscillate ineffectually around the centre in a fashion similar to most of Velasco's regimes. After he had assumed dictatorial powers in 1970, Velasco twice expelled Bucaram from the country to prevent him from campaigning in the elections, and began a smear campaign claiming that Bucaram was foreign-born and not eligible to compete in elections. Velasco's antagonism towards Bucaram can only be interpreted as the old demagogue resenting the popularity of a younger aspirant to his populist mantle. The issue of Bucaram's candidature was finally resolved by the military coup of February 1972, leaving Bucaram to wait in enforced retirement for a possible future election.

The general reaction in Ecuador to the military coup of early 1972 was a sigh of relief. The country was tired of Velasco's corrupt and inefficient regime, and would have welcomed almost any alternative. It was generally recognized that Velasco had been a puppet of the armed forces since his assumption of dictatorial powers in 1970, and the 1972 coup was at first thought to be simply the movement of a back-seat driver into the driving seat. However, the new regime adopted a strongly anti-Velasquista stance, arresting and deporting various leading figures including Velasco himself, and putting two of Velasco's principal ministers up for trial on corruption charges. The regime adopted the title of the 'Revolutionary Nationalist Government' and tried hard to give the impression that a major political transformation had taken place in the country, declaring itself to be 'moral, popular, programatic, anti-feudal, anti-oligarchical, functional and stable' (Brownrigg, 1974, 12). Efficiency and honesty were claimed as the trade-marks of the government, together with the ending of elite rule and foreign domination in Ecuadorian affairs (see GRNE, 1972). A new, radical agrarian reform law, a total reform of the government's bureaucratic operations and a strict control of foreign investments were all promised in the government's first few days of office. Many foreign observers who were not familiar with Ecuadorian politicians' tendency to make wild promises without seriously considering how they can be fulfilled, claimed that the new government represented the new radical style of Latin American military government exemplified by the Velasco Alvarado regime in Peru. As the regime aged, however, it became increasingly apparent that words were not being transformed into deeds and that, in most respects, Ecuador was in a 'carry on as usual' phase, the major differences from previous periods resulting not from the government's actions, but from the effects of oil exports on the economy from August 1972 onwards.

To understand the self-styled 'Revolutionary Nationalist Government', one must understand the personality of its former leader, General Guillermo Rodríguez Lara, a small, rotund man, nicknamed '*bombita*', the 'little bomb'. He originated in Pujilí, a small town in Cotopaxi province, and owns a substantial semi-feudal *hacienda* in that province. Though now a member of the landowning upper class, he had a relatively modest background. In a sense, therefore, he was a self-made man who had been propelled to power by advancement within the armed forces. Indeed, the manners and life-style of Rodríguez and his wife were frequently ridiculed by snobbish members of the Ecuadorian elites as 'brash' and '*nouveau riche*', and even as the habits of 'jumped-up country bumpkins'. Before coming to power, Rodríguez had generally been considered pro-American and he had even received a period of military training in the United States (Brownrigg, 1974, 13). Rodríguez soon proved to be an astute politician, possessing the tact and the ability to handle recalcitrant and ambitious subordinates, which Velasco lacked. At the same time, he possessed Velasco's greatest talent, a liking and capacity for frequent travel and long speech-making. During his Presidency, he travelled throughout the country, addressing an enormous number of mass rallies and meetings of local officials and interest groups. He possessed the major talents of most good political orators: an astute mixture of fiery declarations and emotional commiserations; the ability to imply much while promising little; the ability to talk simultaneously to widely different interest groups, social classes and

57

educational groups, apparently satisfying them all; and the ability patiently to sit through innumerable petitions and boot-licking speeches of praise. Rodríguez adopted Velasco's populist politics, portraying himself as 'a humble man of the people carrying the burdens of the nation', listening to all petitions and demands, paternalistically granting favours and frequently denouncing foreign capitalist interests, national oligarchs, corrupt bureaucrats, speculators, exploitative middlemen and self-seeking politicians.

In its emphasis upon efficiency, honesty and developmentalist policies, the 'Revolutionary Nationalist Government' under Rodríguez was politically similar to the Military Junta of 1963–1966. However, Rodríguez's populist politics and personalistic style of Presidency gave the regime a much more human face than that Junta. In addition, in spite of all its unfulfilled radical promises, the 'Revolutionary Nationalist Government' was enthusiastically supported by some left-wing groups, the most ardent supporters being the Moscow-line Communist party. Left-wing support was particularly obvious for the regime's policies towards the major oil companies up to the middle of 1974. As Ecuador benefited from the oil price rises and increased government participation in oil revenues resulting from the formation of OPEC and the Arab-Israeli war, the government appeared to have the better of the big oil companies. The oil policies were largely the responsibility of Captain Gustavo Jarrín Ampudia, then Minister of Natural Resources, and the best-known member of Rodríguez's government. Jarrín's actions were applauded by left-wing groups in Ecuador and received widespread popular support until oil exports began to drop seriously in the second half of 1974 as Texaco-Gulf put pressure on the Ecuadorian economy and government by reducing production in a period of slack world demand. Jarrín even attained the Presidency of OPEC, and was promoted to rear-admiral in the Ecuadorian navy. His dismissal in the latter part of 1974 marked the beginning of a gradual swing to the political right by the Rodríguez Lara government. This swing was accelerated by an abortive right-wing coup led by General Raúl González Alvear in September 1975. González's rebel troops momentarily captured the Presidential Palace before surrendering to the numerical superiority of troops loyal to the Rodríguez regime. At least two dozen people were killed in the fighting around the Presidential Palace, yet, in the end, González was mysteriously allowed to escape and take asylum

58

in Chile. Immediately after the abortive coup, the government did many of the things which right-wing interests wanted, abolishing a series of measures intended to counter the worsening economic situation and replacing the more radical Ministers in the Cabinet. The full story of this extraordinary attempted coup may never be known. Some even argue that it was a 'pseudo-coup', staged or manipulated to justify a swing to the right by the government.

The abortive September 1975 coup was followed by a period of mounting unpopularity for the government, with increasingly strident demands from the various political parties for elections and a return to civilian rule. Eventually, on January 11th 1976, four months after González's bloody revolt, Rodríguez responded to ministerial and military intrigues, handing power to a three-man Military Junta made up of General Guillermo Durán Arcentales of the army, Vice-Admiral Alfredo Poveda Burbano of the navy and Brigadier-General Luis Leoro Franco of the air force. Both Durán and Poveda were prominent Ministers at different periods of Rodríguez's regime, and Leoro had been exceptionally favoured by Rodríguez in recent air force promotions. Thus, the three members of the Junta which took power after the bloodless coup were all former trusted associates of Rodríguez. The accession of this triumvirate signalled no major policy changes beyond the admission that elections and a return to civilian rule must take place within two years. The removal of Rodríguez had many similarities to the removal of General Velasco Alvarado, the President of Peru, a few months earlier, the main justification used by those taking power being the ending of 'person-alism' and 'erratic decision-making' by the President.

Recent economic changes and their influence on political power relationships

Five economic and social effects of military rule in Ecuador since 1972 are worthy of special mention: the enormous growth in imports, including luxuries; the acceleration of industrialization; the growth in the armed forces' participation in activities outside the fields of government and military activity; the great increase in cooperatives; and the considerable growth in state control of various sectors of the national economy.

When the 'Revolutionary Nationalist Government' took power in 1972, it was naturally concerned not to arouse opposition. Given the prevalent opinion that Ecuador's most pressing problems would be solved within a few months by the inflow of oil revenues, there was no strong emphasis on the internal mobilization of resources, the promotion of Ecuadorian capital investment, or the establishment of a policy of austerity and self-sacrifice. Consumption was not restrained, and the consumption of some imported luxury goods was actually increased by the lowering of certain import duties. By mid-1975, after less than three years of a strong positive trade balance resulting from the new oil exports, imports had caught up with exports again. Of course, much of this growth in imports was the purchase of capital equipment and raw materials for agriculture and industry, but a large part was the importation of unnecessary gadgets, luxury consumer goods, and excessively expensive vehicles and office equipment. The 1972–1975 period saw the mass appearance of new, luxury cars in Quito and Guayaquil, the opulent refurnishing of many government offices, and the installation of stereo sets and other prestige symbols in the offices of many senior executives and civil servants. It also saw a great improvement in the equipment and uniforms of much of the armed forces and police. It was, in short, a period of unrestrained consumption, bringing the 'oil boom' to a premature end in 1975.

Linked to the rapid expansion of imports in the 1972–1975 period was an impressive growth in industrial investment and output. The government's relatively favourable attitude towards foreign investment, combined with Ecuador's political stability and good economic prospects in the 1972–75 period, induced both foreign and Ecuadorian interests to invest heavily in new factories and industrial equipment. Most of this industrialization was light engineering, assembling foreign components and relying upon foreign patents, to supply the Ecuadorian market and a limited number of consumers in other countries of the Andean Group. Industrial output grew in value by 14% in 1973, and by 15% in 1974 (*BOLSA Review*, vol 9, 1975, 595), reflecting the exceptionally rapid growth of the sector. It should be remembered, however, that this was the growth of one of the smallest

60

industrial systems in South America. Industrialization caused a heavy increase in imports of equipment and raw materials, as well as a rapid inflow of foreign investment, totalling 32.7 million dollars in 1974 and 90.5 million dollars in 1975 (BOLSA Review, vol 10, 1976, 220). Besides the well-known problems of import substitution industrialization in small, economically and technologically dependent countries (see Boorstein, 1968, 5–7; Weeks, 1972, 61–6), the industrialization process diverted much potential investment away from other sectors. In 1974, for example, manufacturing accounted for 75% of foreign investment and 72% of total Ecuadorian public and private investment, contributing indirectly to the stagnation of agriculture, whose output only grew in value by 1% in 1973, and by 2% in 1974 (BOLSA Review, vol 9, 1975, 595).

During the 1960s, the Ecuadorian armed forces, like most other armed forces in Latin America, were strengthened and re-equipped in the effusion of United States' aid which accompanied the Alliance for Progress and the associated drive to counter left-wing subversion. In the 1970s, the military strength and prestige of the Ecuadorian armed forces have been further increased by the use of government oil revenues to improve military salaries and to purchase new equipment. This military strengthening of the armed forces has been accompanied by an increasing participation in government. Since the overthrow of Velasco in 1961, the armed forces have either formed the government or pulled the strings behind the government for most of the 15 years through to 1976. This has been the most significant period of military dominance of Ecuadorian politics in the twentieth century. Senior military officers are now accustomed to occupying posts as Ministers, department heads, provincial governors, inspectors and auditors, and more junior military personnel are used to being called upon to perform work normally done by police and local officials. The training of military officers has been adapted to include courses for potential administrators and policy makers and many military personnel are decidedly reluctant to be 'sent back to barracks'. The armed forces have been granted substantial areas of land for urban housing schemes and rural colonization projects, and whole neighbourhoods are now inhabited by serving and retired military personnel. The armed forces have also invested in various industries and transport enterprises, including their own commercial airline (TAME), their own merchant fleet (TRASNAVE), their own fleet of oil tankers

(FLOPEC), and their own shipyards (ASTINAVE). They even have their own farms, hospitals and schools and their own import-export and wholesaling and retailing systems. Thus, they are becoming increasingly embedded in almost all aspects of political, economic and social activity, forming a virtual 'State within a State'.

From the late 1960s onwards, it became Ecuadorian government policy to encourage or force small enterprises to group together in cooperatives. This attitude resulted largely from the criticisms levelled at the 1964 Agrarian Reform Law and the subsequent decrees abolishing precarious forms of land tenure, which gave *hacienda* serfs title to some of the land they worked. These measures produced a great increase in the number of *minifundia* in the country, and a break-down in the old paternalistic relations between the *hacienda* and its workers. Pressure grew to agglomerate small farmers into cooperatives which could more effectively modernize their operations and link up with government institutions. This was partially achieved by a series of decrees and laws, culminating in the 1973 Agrarian Reform Law produced by the 'Revolutionary Nationalist Govern-ment'. The legal pressure to form cooperatives in Ecuador has been very successful, not just amongst small farmers, but also amongst transporters and some groups of artisans and consumers. Effectively, the government refuses to deal with individuals who are not members of cooperatives. Thus, most small farmer credit is issued to coopera-tives, land titles in colonization zones are normally only sold to members of cooperatives and bus drivers are only authorized to work a particular route if they are members of cooperatives. While there were only 485 cooperatives in Ecuador in 1960, this number had increased to 2,274 in 1973, with a total of over 100,000 members (Hurtado and Herudek, 1974, 34–5). Since 1973, the number of cooperatives has increased even more rapidly as a result of the gradual application of the 1973 Agrarian Reform Law in selected priority zones. Unfortunately, however, the basic principle of the cooperative, 'cooperation', has been secondary to the legal constraints which force many small enterprises to join cooperatives. The development of cooperatives has frequently had little effect in encouraging communal labour or the harmonious sharing of equipment and facilities, but it has had one overwhelming important effect, to tie small enterprises to the benevolent paternalism of the State (see Hurtado and Herudek, 1974, 52–8; Ortiz, 1975, 97–122). In many senses, the State has replaced the *hacienda* owner as the principal patron of the rural poor. This tendency has been particularly accentuated by the use of oil revenues since 1972 to increase the provision of credits to all types of enterprises (see Table 2).

The strengthening of the socio-economic powers of the State through the enforced formation of cooperatives is paralleled by an increasing government participation in a wide variety of different sectors of the economy. For decades, the Ecuadorian government has tended to concentrate its capital investments in the provision of roads, electricity supply, water supply and other forms of infrastructure, but, particularly since 1972, it has moved into the ownership of many other types of enterprise. Oil revenues have been used to buy an increasing stake in oil production and marketing, to construct a state oil refinery near Esmeraldas and even to finance exploratory drilling for oil (see Kendall, 1975). These ventures have been handled by a State oil corporation, CEPE,[21] founded in 1972, which has rapidly grown into the largest Ecuadorian economic enterprise. It is involved in the extraction of natural gas from the Gulf of Guayaquil, and is considering ventures into the fertilizer and petrochemical industries. Furthermore, it is gradually increasing its share of oil refining and fuel distribution and retailing in the country, taking over from Anglo-Ecuadorian Oilfields and Gulf Oil, the main companies handling distribution to Ecuadorian consumers. Many of Ecuador's new industrial enterprises are 'mixed companies', combining elements of foreign, private and government capital. The government has also developed its own storage, wholesaling and retailing system for many products and has increased its effective control over many private companies and *haciendas* through the provision of greatly increased credit. Thus, mainly through the use of oil revenues, the government has rapidly increased its share in the national economy and its influence over the remainder of the economy.

Since 1972, significant changes in the distribution of political power in Ecuador have resulted from the rapid increase in imports, the acceleration of industrialization, the increase in the economic power of the armed forces, the promotion of cooperatives and the penetration of the State into more and more parts of the economy. Relatively speaking, the large landowners and the Church have declined in political importance, while the import-export merchants

---

21 *Corporación Estatal Petrolera Ecuatoriana.*

and urban property owners and industrialists have increased in importance. Most significant of all, however, has been the entrenchment of the armed forces in almost all parts of the economic and governmental system and the enormous growth in government ownership and/or control of many sectors of the economy. Senior military officers and civil servants have become much more powerful *vis-à-vis* other elite groups. The scope for government intervention in, and management of, the economy and society has been greatly increased. Correspondingly, however, there has been an increase in the potential scale of government bureaucracy and paternalism, and in the opportunities for government-mediated dependence upon foreign interests and pressures.

CHAPTER IV

Planning in Ecuador
Since 1950

THE COMBINATION OF continual economic uncertainty, chronic political instability, strong local and inter-regional rivalries and marked social divisions, makes Ecuador a particularly difficult country in which to undertake long-term planning. In spite of this, various minor attempts at planning were made in the thirties and forties (see JNPC, 1966, 8–11; Zuvekas, 1972, 2–6; Salvador, 1974, 3–6), and, since the early fifties, a considerable number of national, regional and local development plans have been prepared and a complex civil service bureaucracy has been established for planning. This planning seems to have been attempted more because of international pressures than because of any serious Ecuadorian belief in the virtues of planned development. Almost all foreign advisors and development banks have strongly recommended planning, and, in many cases, the preparation of comprehensive development plans has been a precondition for the receipt of economic aid.

As in most Latin American countries, the establishment and growth of a national planning system in Ecuador is closely related to the activities of international organizations within the United Nations and Interamerican groupings (see Lahmeyer Lobo, 1966, 341–4), and to the encouragement of the United States government. The initial stimulus to the establishment of a national planning system came from the United Nations Economic Commission for Latin America (UNECLA), which, in January 1954, produced a comprehensive study of the Ecuadorian economy with projections and suggested investment strategies. This study had the special aim of stimulating further research and of initiating a national economic planning system. Mainly as a result of UNECLA's efforts, and with some encouragement from the World Bank, Ecuador established a National Planning

Board[22] in May 1954 (see Salvador, 1974, 6–9). From a small organization with less than two dozen staff in 1954, the National Planning Board has gradually developed into a major government department with a staff now approaching 300. Since its foundation, the Board has received considerable technical assistance from UNECLA and from the related Latin American Institute of Economic and Social Planning (known as ILPES), institutions which are based in Santiago, Chile. The preparation of each major plan in Ecuador has been accompanied by an invasion of UNECLA and ILPES consultants, and sometimes also by consultants from the United Nations organizations based in New York. The major development banks, and particularly the World Bank (International Bank for Reconstruction and Development) and the Inter-American Development Bank, have also frequently intervened in Ecuador's planning system to promote particular projects, to press home offers of funding and to insist on detailed pre-project evaluation studies. In addition, the Organization of American States, particularly since the establishment of the Alliance for Progress in 1961, has been heavily involved in promoting, advising, and even financing planning in Ecuador. It is no secret that the Alliance for Progress was not so much a hemispheric programme or alliance, as a United States government programme to reverse the spread of Communist influence in Latin America in the early 1960s. Inevitably, the activities of the World Bank, Inter-American Development Bank and Organization of American States, all based in Washington DC, have been closely linked to foreign policy objectives of the United States, and to the advisory and financial roles of the United States Agency for International Development (USAID). The result of such a high degree of foreign intervention in Ecuador's national planning structure has been the imposition of foreign styles, techniques and objectives upon the nascent Ecuadorian planning system. This situation has been accentuated by the fact that many of Ecuador's most senior planners have been trained in other Latin American countries, in the United States, or in Western Europe. Inevitably, the high degree of foreign assistance and intervention in the planning process has encouraged the rapid growth and increasing sophistication of Ecuadorian planning. However, it has failed to stimulate any effective self-evaluation process on the part of Ecuador's

---

[22] *Junta Nacional de Planificación y Coordinación Económica,* abbreviated as JNPC or JUNAPLA.

decision-makers and politicians, or any deep-rooted desire for planning on the part of Ecuador's population. The seed of planning in Ecuador has been carefully watered and fertilized by foreign organizations, but the eventual product has failed to integrate itself effectively into the local ecosystem.

Attitudes to planning and impediments to its effectiveness

In terms of performance, planning in Ecuador has been almost totally ineffective. There has been no successful linkage between the planning bureaucracy and the executive sections of the government, so that almost no plan has been fully implemented and most plans have not been used at all. Calling for the preparation of a development plan has become a means for the government in power to put off any unwanted action while satisfying foreign and national interests that suitable steps are being taken. Generally, by the time the plan is finally ready, a change of government or a reshuffle in the relevant ministry has occurred, so that the plan is never implemented. Even if no such change occurs, it is a frequent ploy for politicians to accuse the planners of incompetence or corruption and to order a new plan, so postponing action even further. Many Ecuadorians take a certain pride in the 'happy-go-lucky' nature of Ecuador's 'Latin' traditions, and methodical 'Anglo-Saxon' planning is considered more a matter for ridicule than for admiration. Some scholars believe that the Ecuadorian national temperament is more suited to an impulsive, charismatic leadership than to any cold, calculating assessment of long-term aims and investment strategies. It is often pointed out that Europe's tremendous nineteenth-century economic expansion was essentially unplanned, and that even today many of the capitalist developed countries do not engage in long-term comprehensive economic planning.

The widespread distrust of planning in Ecuador and the frequent use of plans and planners as 'political footballs' rather than as a means of accelerating national development has had very serious consequences. Planning is relatively expensive, and the maintenance of the Ecuadorian civil service planners and the foreign planning consultants has placed

67

a considerable burden on the Ecuadorian taxpayer and has led to increased borrowing abroad by the Ecuadorian government. In spite of paying for planning, however, Ecuador has suffered all the disadvantages of an unplanned country. The failure to implement suitable priorities for long-term investment has meant that scarce funds have often been dissipated on a multitude of uncoordinated and often unnecessary projects which may never be finished. Perhaps the most striking example of this is the attempt, since the 1920s, to link the Andean highlands with the eastern lowlands by road. The division of funds and effort between over thirty different routes meant that it was not until 1947 that the first road was completed, and not until 1960 that the second road was finished. Even today there are only four complete roads. The remaining unfinished roads are at present virtually useless and lie abandoned or are being extended eastward by only one or two kilometres a year (see Bromley, 1972, 281–2). Such wastage of scarce financial resources and manpower is inexcusable when the choice of a few priority routes for road construction and the concentration of funds and effort on these routes would have enabled a more rapid and complete integration of the eastern lowlands into the national economy. Throughout Ecuador there are a remarkable number of abandoned and unfinished public works which bear witness to the need for planned development to avoid wastage of resources.

The chronic problem of Ecuadorian planning has been an over-concentration on the mechanics and bureaucracy of planning, and a lack of attention to plan implementation. This problem is common to many less-developed countries, and particularly to those of Latin America. These countries are saturated with 'paper planning', the preparation of plans which have no real chance of implementation. In some cases, the plans simply fail to specify a workable system of implementation. Even if such a system of implementation is specified, the plan's achievement may be frustrated by lack of cooperation from executive agencies, or conditions of economic or political instability may make the plan's targets unrealistic. When a plan's targets are achieved, this is not necessarily a result of the plan and its implementation. The achievement of planned targets may simply be a chance result of normal changes. In a situation of 'paper planning', the good planner may be simply a good forecaster; a person who estimates what growth is likely to occur and who incorporates these estimates

68

into the plans as targets. If the forecasts are accurate, the plan's targets will be achieved even though the plan is never implemented. Sometimes, 'paper planning' may be so oriented towards the completion of the plan document itself that the eventual achievement of the plan's objectives loses all significance. Cacho (1975, 42) describes this situation as follows:

> 'Planning is too often regarded, even today, as little more than the act of preparing a multi-year document called a plan. When this approach is adopted, the plan becomes an end in itself rather than a means to achieve development; it is usually not operationally oriented, and little attempt is made to implement it'.

Griffin and Enos (1970, 201) point to the political significance of plans as 'publicity documents' and advertisements for a regime's policies, and as means of attracting foreign loans and investments. Discussing the failure of Colombia to implement its 1961–71 General Plan for Economic and Social Development, they pose a question which could equally well be applied to any of Ecuador's national plans, and which would receive the same answer:

> 'Should the plan be considered a failure? That depends upon one's point of view. As an exercise in the making of economic policy the plan has certainly been a failure; no attempt has been made to implement it and its targets are not being achieved. On the other hand, the plan was conceived not as an economic document, but as a political document, as an exercise in diplomacy. It was a way of dramatizing the problems and aspirations of Colombia to the rest of the world and a means of establishing a claim for aid from the United States under the Alliance for Progress programme. As a diplomatic manoeuvre for attracting foreign capital the plan was a success. . . . In spite of the fact that the plan had no influence on policy, . . . one cannot say that economic planning has failed in Colombia; it has never been tried'.

Further on (Griffin and Enos, 1970, 203), the same authors generalize about planning in Latin America.

> 'Where plans exist, they are frequently prepared by foreign technicians working with a few local advisors. The plans are essentially technocratic exercises. The general public does not participate in choosing the plan's objectives, and as a consequence, the plans enjoy little general support. The plans are not implemented, nor are they intended to be implemented. They are documents prepared largely by foreigners, for foreigners'.

Each one of these descriptions of 'paper planning' applies to Ecuador even more than to most of the larger Latin American countries.

Ecuadorian development planning has essentially been an elite and technocratic exercise conducted to give governments a status symbol policy document and to attract foreign loans and investment. Thus, Ecuadorian planning has closely reflected Ecuador's dependency upon foreign finance and technical expertise, and has involved no significant participation of the Ecuadorian population, and no great commitment to social change or the redeployment of resources on the part of Ecuador's elites. Planning has become a prestige, high-status occupation, superior to most other forms of governmental or academic activity, and commanding respect in its own right. The result has been to convert planning into a symbolic charade, or, to use the term of Griffin and Enos, a 'facade' for a lack of effective, organized activity on the part of government.

In many senses, it is unfair to blame Ecuador's successive governments for the irrelevance and ineffectiveness of planning. They simply followed the models of planning proposed by international agencies, and these agencies were at fault in stressing planning technique at the expense of plan implementation and in recommending a style of planning that was totally inappropriate to open dependent capitalist economies like that of Ecuador. The system of fixed-term five- and ten-year plans prescribing long-term targets is relatively well suited to 'command economies' with a high degree of autonomy from changing international situations, such as the countries of the Soviet Block, but it is far too inflexible to cope with 'mixed economies' in small Latin American countries. Ecuador's susceptibility to changes in the terms of international trade, to fluctuations in crop production and to political instability, all point in the direction of shorter term, more flexible planning systems such as rolling three-year plans, with continuous monitoring, evaluation and adjustment. In such a system, planning would have to be closely linked to budget allocation and to project and programme implementation. Longer-term planning would be limited to the determination of key long-term targets, priorities and allocations, so that shorter-term progress could be related to broad long-term objectives. Cacho (1975, 42) describes such an ideal type of planning as:

> 'a continuous process in which government plays a management role in mobilizing the society and collaborating with it in a complex assortment of activities based on the plan and geared to attaining its objectives. A plan should be regarded as a living instrument, flexible and evolving in

response to changes in the numerous assumptions on which its direction, policies and programs are based. It should not be a once-and-for-all purely reference document of fixed prescriptions for the period to be covered'.

Unfortunately, Ecuadorian planning has, to date, been the exact opposite of Cacho's desired planning system. Popular participation in the planning process has not been effectively encouraged, and popular participation in the achievement of planned objectives has received little official consideration. 'Social mobilization' is considered a dangerous process by Ecuador's rulers, and the usual hope of government is that the masses will passively and gratefully accept the development which is handed down to them by the State. The result has been a technocratic planning process with little more than token consultation of national, regional and provincial elites, and no effective consultation of peasants' or workers' organizations. In turn, of course, the plans have had little popular understanding or support.

The response of government to the widespread apathy towards planning and planners has generally been a form of 'anti-planning', the concession of special assistance to particular interest groups, whether or not these concessions correspond to planned targets. Particularly under Velasco Ibarra and Rodríguez Lara, the two greatest populist Presidents since 1950, the Presidency has been converted into 'a roving trouble-shooting service', travelling from town to town, attending carefully stage-managed pro-government meetings, listening to local grievances and aspirations and paternalistically granting favours to local elites. Thus, for example, a national plan may deliberately avoid the inclusion of a particular road or irrigation scheme because such a scheme does not correspond to a national set of priorities. However, on visiting the area concerned, the President listens to local petitions and grants that the scheme will be implemented. As a result, a further scheme is added to the nation's overloaded budgeting and implementation system, meaning that either a higher priority will be neglected, or that all projects will proceed towards completion at a slower rate. Even when the President does not visit particular areas, delegations from those areas may visit Quito to plead their case. In general, the inability of the President and his Ministers to say 'no', means that public investment programmes are continuously being expanded far beyond planned targets and the nation's ability to pay, or to execute the programmes.

71

This almost continuous process of addition to existing plans is not only a reflection of politicians' failings, but also of the deficiencies of existing plans resulting from the metropolitan attitudes and techocratic approach of most Ecuadorian planners. The National Planning Board is not a place for muddy boots and most of its planners rarely travel outside the largest cities and their immediate environs. If visits to remote and peripheral areas of the country take place at all, they are usually restricted to a very few days, and consultations are normally limited to discussions with local officials and elites. Most senior government officials in Ecuador have stronger links with large cities in other countries than with the urban slums or rural areas of *minifundia* in their own country. There is a real ignorance of the squalid living conditions and physical and social isolation of Ecuador's poor, and as a result, there is an inbuilt tendency towards technocratic, futuristic planning and towards the establishment of prestige projects such as the proposed Quito–Guayaquil motorway, and the extravagant urban renewal proposals for Quito and Guayaquil. Even when development programmes are oriented towards the poor, the programmes are frequently planned and implemented in a paternalistic and bureaucratic fashion and, as a result, they have little success. Indeed, the groups who profit from such programmes are often the bureaucrats and contractors who implement the programmes, and the local middle classes, rather than the poor themselves. Typical examples of such failures are Ecuador's half-hearted attempts at agrarian reform and at programmes to help the highland Indian population. The failures of these programmes reflect the failure of many government officials to identify and effectively tackle the roots of poverty and exploitation. Not only can planning itself be called a charade, but also much of plan implementation, because of the alienation of planners and bureaucrats from the groups that they are seeking to affect.

The institutional position of the National Planning Board

The preceding section reflects how easy it is to criticize planners in Ecuador. Some of the criticisms that have been made, and many more, are repeated daily by Ecuadorians of different political leanings.

To be fair, however, many Ecuadorian planners recognize most of these problems, but are unable to tackle them because of their own situation in the government. In any conglomeration of organizations, critical members tend to be over-ruled and even thrown out by the other members, and many of the National Planning Board's recommendations to the Ecuadorian government are simply ignored. The Board is put under continuous pressure by demands from the Presidency to incorporate more and more elements into plans and programmes, these demands often reflecting nothing more than blatant pressure from elite minority groups. The other sections of the Ecuadorian government tend to resent the Board becoming involved in plan implementation, claiming that the Board's task is only to plan, and not to become involved in executing its ideas. The Board's official terms of reference prohibit the institution from assuming a central role in the execution of planned developments, and institutional rivalries lead other sections of government to resent the intrusion of the Board in anything more than an advisory capacity. In a few cases, Board staff have even been denied the information necessary to monitor and evaluate programmes executed by other government departments.

The most significant traditional tendency in Ecuador's government is the tendency for personal and institutional rivalries to cause the proliferation of government institutions, many of them autonomous and effectively outside any hierarchical structure (see JNPC, 1973; Brownrigg, 1974, 7). Just as political parties in Ecuador have almost continuously divided and sub-divided, even when there is no real ideological difference, so government institutions have proliferated, even though many overlap with one another, and most are hopelessly impoverished of resources. The result is a complex and deeply-divided bureaucracy which would require a very powerful Planning Board to give any effective coordination or coherence. In reality, however, the Board's position within the government is decidedly precarious and rather ineffectively defined, so that the Board cannot realistically coordinate government activities. The Board is officially a planning and coordinating agency attached to the Secretariat of the Presidency of the Republic. The President of the Planning Board has Cabinet status, but the Planning Board is not equivalent to a Ministry of Planning, nor to a Directorate superior to all Ministries. Instead, its position is deliberately ambiguous.

The Board is more powerful and respected than the less prestigious Ministries, such as the Ministries of Labour and Health, but it is weaker than the more powerful and established Ministries, such as the Ministries of Defence, Public Works, Finance and Agriculture. Because the Planning Board is relatively weak in these higher circles of government, and because there is no alternative institution to give the government a coherent focus, each Ministry tends to go its own way according to the whims and policy orientations of its senior personnel. Most Ministers are concerned to further their own political careers and try to give their administrations a distinctive personalistic stamp, resisting the attempts of the Planning Board to impose a common policy orientation throughout the government. Thus, just as 'personalism' has prevented the development of class solidarity in Ecuadorian politics, this same personalism has impeded the development of institutional solidarity in the Ecuadorian government.

The prestige attached to planning in Ecuador has meant that most government departments have been reluctant to leave all planning to the National Planning Board. Most major government departments have prepared their own sectoral 'paper plans', frequently overlapping, and sometimes conflicting, with the plans prepared by the Planning Board. The result has been a waste of effort and resources in planning, the proliferation of overlapping and impoverished projects and a lack of adequate attention to plan implementation, monitoring and evaluation.

The predicament of the Planning Board could be resolved relatively easily by giving the Board control over the allocation of all government finance. However, though the Board plays a nominal role in this process, the Ministry of Finance and the Central Bank are reluctant to give up the key positions of power that they hold within the government. As a result, the Board is relegated to a peripheral position in national financial decision-making, and is unable to insist that only projects and programmes within the national plans can receive government financing. Each government department feels that it has the right to spend its allocation as it wishes, and to request additional funds without making itself accountable to the Planning Board for its expenditure. The main financial powers of the Planning Board have, therefore, been exercised at a rather low level of government, the approval of the annual budgets of provincial councils and cantonal authorities. At this level, the Planning Board has notionally been able to insist upon compliance with national planning objectives. However, this supervision has generally proved ineffective because of the unfamiliarity of provincial and cantonal authorities with efficient accounting procedures, and because of the Board's inability to supervise entities outside Quito closely. In many cases, provincial and cantonal authorities simply 'cook the books' so as to ensure that their programmes can go ahead when the Planning Board would wish to stop them. Thus, for example, the Planning Board's repeated pleas for greater expenditure on road maintenance and on the completion of existing projects are often simply ignored in favour of the initiation of new road projects which will probably never be completed.

When the Planning Board has tried to impose its ideas upon recalcitrant politicians, the result has generally been the dismissal of one or more senior members of the Planning Board. The division between 'technocrats' and 'politicians' within the Ecuadorian government has always been strong, and, if anything, it has widened over the last decade as the 'technocrats' have acquired more sophisticated equipment and techniques. Just as in North America and Western Europe (see Catanese, 1974), the professional planner has tended to become more and more immersed in technical issues and long-term prognoses because he is effectively unable to influence short-term policy making. Planners have generally been subservient to politicians and have found their own growing technical expertise and evaluative skill increasingly in conflict with the politician's intuitive and personalistic approach. The result has been for planners to retreat into a technocratic dream-world, separating themselves from government decision-making and plan implementation so as to preserve their own intellectual and moral integrity, and more importantly, to save their own jobs. Even within the Planning Board, the relations between planners and politicians are often somewhat strained. The most important figure in the institution is the President of the Board, a person who is generally a political appointee with little or no technical knowledge or expertise. So as to give the Board a specialist orientation, the second most important figure is the Technical Director, who is generally a career economist with strong academic and technocratic leanings. Very often, the President and the Technical Director form opposite poles within the Board, each heading their own hierarchies. The President heads a bureaucratic and political hierarchy including the general administration of the Board, the personnel department, the accounts department, and so on, while the Technical Director heads his own technical hierarchy, including the various subdirectorates, divisions and sections of the Board. The polarization between the President and the Technical Director tends to lead to conflicts within the Board, and to frequent dismissals and resignations. The general instability of the national government further accentuates this process, so that a Presidency or Technical Directorship in the National Planning Board may change hands as many as four times in a single year during a period of political instability. Changes of senior government officials in Ecuador are generally much more frequent than changes of Presidents of the Republic, reflecting the President of the Republic's power to sack or rotate Cabinet members and other senior government personnel, using those individuals as scapegoats for the failure of government policies. Naturally, such a situation is highly disruptive in a coordinating and planning institution like the National Planning Board. The middle level personnel in the Board, such as the divisional and sectional chiefs and their main assistants, generally hold their posts for relatively long periods and possess considerable experience. However, they are prevented from working efficiently by the frequency of changes at the higher levels, each higher level change being accompanied by weeks or even months of uncertainty. Power within the Board is heavily concentrated upon the President, and middle-level personnel usually dare not take independent action without Presidential support. Those who become exasperated by the delays and uncertainties of political control of the planning process tend to resign or to be dismissed, so that the Board tends to lose any middle-level personnel, and even any Technical Director, who is capable of effective independent action.

Figure 5 (based on JNPC, 1973, 68) shows the structure of the National Planning Board in 1975. This complex structure has two almost separate hierarchies, one dependent upon the President, and the other upon the Technical Director. The President exercises overall control over the Technical Director and his personnel, and the Directorate has a notional control over the whole Board. In 1973, the Directorate was composed of the following members: the President of the National Planning Board (nominated by the President of the Republic); the Minister of Finance; the Minister of Agriculture

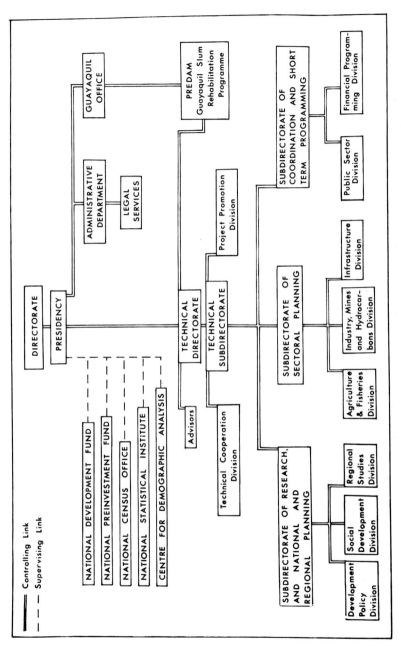

Controlling Link
Supervising Link

DIRECTORATE

PRESIDENCY

ADMINISTRATIVE DEPARTMENT

LEGAL SERVICES

GUAYAQUIL OFFICE

PREDAM Guayaquil Slum Rehabilitation Programme

NATIONAL DEVELOPMENT FUND

NATIONAL PREINVESTMENT FUND

NATIONAL CENSUS OFFICE

NATIONAL STATISTICAL INSTITUTE

CENTRE FOR DEMOGRAPHIC ANALYSIS

Advisors

TECHNICAL DIRECTORATE

TECHNICAL SUBDIRECTORATE

Technical Cooperation Division

Project Promotion Division

SUBDIRECTORATE OF RESEARCH, AND NATIONAL AND REGIONAL PLANNING

SUBDIRECTORATE OF SECTORAL PLANNING

SUBDIRECTORATE OF COORDINATION AND SHORT TERM PROGRAMMING

Development Policy Division

Social Development Division

Regional Studies Division

Agriculture & Fisheries Division

Industry, Mines and Hydrocarbons Division

Infrastructure Division

Public Sector Division

Financial Programming Division

FIGURE 5: THE STRUCTURE OF THE NATIONAL PLANNING BOARD IN 1975

and Livestock Raising; the Minister of Industry, Commerce and Integration; the Minister of Natural Resources and Energy; the Minister of Public Works; the General Manager of the Central Bank; the General Manager of the National Development Bank (*Banco Nacional de Fomento*); and one representative for the agricultural sector, one for the industrial sector and one for the commercial sector, these representatives being chosen by the Chambers of Agriculture, Industry and Commerce, the institutions which represent the interests of large landowners, industrialists and import-export merchants to the government. Even though the representatives of the Chambers of Agriculture, Industry and Commerce do not have voting rights, their presence ensures an upper-class control over the National Planning Board's activities, providing a major obstacle to the Board proposing any effective redistributive policies for the country. The existence of the Directorate of the Planning Board simply adds yet another level to a desperately overcrowded administrative hierarchy. It is far from clear why, when half of the National Cabinet is on the Directorate of the Planning Board, the Cabinet cannot assume the role of the Directorate, so eliminating an unnecessary administrative level. The President of the National Planning Board sits on the Directorates of at least 29 other government institutions (JNPC, 1975a, 8). In theory, such a role enables the National Planning Board effectively to coordinate all government departments and to ensure that its plans are implemented. Regrettably, however, most of these Directorates have five to fifteen members, and the opinion of the President of the National Planning Board commands no greater respect than that of the various Ministries which are represented. As a result, these bureaucratic committees consume a substantial part of the time of the President of the National Planning Board without yielding any major benefit to the planning system. The only effect tends to be that the Board suffers from an 'absentee President' who has insufficient time to deal with his intra-institutional responsibilities.

The structure of the Planning Board and the composition of its Directorate both indicate a further deficiency of the Ecuadorian national planning system: the dominance of economic planning over social, regional and physical planning, and the corresponding dominance of economics graduates in the Planning Board. At its highest levels, the National Planning Board has traditionally been dominated by politicians and economists, with the assistance of civil engineers and lawyers. The shortage of personnel trained in public administration and political science has encouraged the divorce between planning and plan implementation, and the lack of popular participation in the planning process. The shortage of sociologists, anthropologists and social administrators has encouraged the neglect of social mobilization and special programmes to assist marginal groups. The shortage of architects and regional scientists has encouraged the neglect of regional development problems and physical planning problems. As a result of these deficiencies, economic planning has had little chance of success. Each economic programme has been frustrated by the lack of appropriate human resources, public apathy, the failure to choose suitable locations, and the failure of different institutions to coordinate with one another to achieve the programme's objective. Development has tended to be accompanied by a widening of socio-economic and inter-regional disparities, often weakening, rather than strengthening, the country's long-term potential. Although such problems could possibly be resolved by more and better economists, it would be more rational to develop a balanced, inter-disciplinary planning team adopting a unified approach (see UNRISD, 1973) to development planning, giving equal prominence to economic, social, regional and physical objectives.

It is perhaps fitting to conclude this section with a note of sympathy for the staff of the National Planning Board. Velasco Ibarra's oft-repeated truism that 'Ecuador is a very difficult country to govern' (see Martz, 1972, 1) might be rewritten as 'Ecuador is a very difficult country to plan', one of the greatest obstacles to planning being Velasco Ibarra himself and the impulsive, charismatic, personalistic style of leadership that he typifies. Ecuador simply does not have the institutional or political climate necessary for planning to be effective. Minor improvements to the planning system have been achieved in recent years, but these represent only the first faltering steps towards an effective system. The main achievements since 1971 have been the strengthening of the data collection and data processing institutions attached to the Planning Board, and the establishment of two major government financial agencies, FONAPRE, the National Preinvestment Fund, and FONADE, the National Development Fund, loosely attached to the Planning Board. FONADE and FONAPRE are designed to utilize oil revenues to finance feasibility studies and initial investments in major development projects. They give the Board some control over one aspect of national financial allocations. Another tentative step towards increasing the Board's powers has been the establishment in 1975 of PREDAM, the rehabilitation plan for the marginal slum areas of Guayaquil, in which the Planning Boards plays a coordinating role in a multi-institutional project, going closer than the Board has ever gone before towards a real executive role. Even more important is the growing interest within the Planning Board in the establishment of a system of short-term, rolling national plans and in the creation of a regional planning system. Although both of these ideas will take some time to reach fruition, they should help to make planning a more efficient and relevant exercise. Most of these recent extensions of the Board's powers and interests reflect the growth in governmental powers and activities in Ecuador since major oil exports began in 1972.

Integral national plans

Since its establishment in 1954, the National Planning Board has produced five national plans (JNPC, 1958, 1961, 1963, 1969b and 1972).

The Board's first national development plan in 1958 was entitled 'Bases and directives for the economic development of Ecuador' and was intended to provide a complete national plan for the period 1959–1965, and some general guidelines up to 1990. The plan concentrated mainly on agriculture and industry and devoted relatively short sections to electrification and education. Almost no consideration was given to mining, forestry, fishing, transport, land tenure, colonization, social structure or regional planning, and the plan failed to specify any investment targets or other financial details. This first, and very unsatisfactory, attempt at national planning was almost completely ignored by the government.

The Board's second national plan in 1961 was entitled 'Immediate development plan', and was intended to cover the period 1961–1963 as an interim plan before the publication of the third plan, to cover the period 1964–1973. The second plan managed to remedy many of the principal omissions and defects of the first plan, and it produced detailed targets for government investment concentrated particularly in the fields of transport, education and agricultural development. The plan was based upon an estimated annual growth in gross domestic product of 5.3% (JNPC, 1961, I, 60), but in reality this growth rate was not achieved and the plan was only partially implemented.

The third plan, entitled 'General plan for the economic and social development of Ecuador, 1964–1973', was a far more detailed and competent study than either of the two preceding plans. It relied upon an average annual growth in gdp of 6.5% over the whole ten-year period (Zuvekas, 1972, 51), and specified the government and private investment distribution given in Table 11. The plan was highly praised by an international team of experts sent by the Alliance for Progress (Committee of Nine, 1965, 5–8), and it was adopted by the military government of 1963–66 as the basis for Ecuadorian development policy (JNPC, 1964b, 4). Until the fall of the military junta in

TABLE 11

GOVERNMENT AND PRIVATE INVESTMENT SPECIFIED IN THE THIRD
NATIONAL PLAN, 1964–1973

Expressed as percentages of the total ten-year expenditure

Calculated from data in Committee of Nine (1964, 100, table III-9).

	Government Investment %	Private Investment %	Total Investment %
Agriculture, fisheries and forestry ...	11.3	29.2	21.6
Mining and petroleum	0.4	4.3	2.6
Industry	3.4	27.5	17.3
Construction	0.1	3.5	2.1
Electrification	24.1	2.9	11.8
Transport and telecommunications	31.4	6.1	16.8
Education, housing and health ...	20.1	22.4	21.5
Others	9.2	4.1	6.3
TOTAL (%)	100.0	100.0	100.0
Total ten-year expenditure in millions of sucres at 1963 prices...	19,325.7	26,472.4	45,798.1

1966, the plan was taken relatively seriously by the government, but after 1966, it was virtually abandoned (Zuvekas, 1972, 55). In 1964, the first year of the plan's operation, the actual growth in gdp was higher than that predicted in the plan. From 1965 onwards, however, it fell well short of the planned growth, and, by 1968, a serious balance-of-payments crisis was developing, due mainly to the decline in banana exports.

The political and economic obstacles to the implementation of the ten-year plan led the National Planning Board to prepare a fourth national plan in 1969, entitled 'The development of Ecuador, 1970–1973'. This plan was essentially a modification of the third plan with special provisions to relieve the balance-of-payments crisis. It was based upon an estimated average annual growth in gdp of 8.4% (JNPC, 1969b, I, 435), and fixed the government investment distribution given in Table 12. Unfortunately, the investment targets are not fully comparable with those of the third plan because of changes in the classification of categories of expenditure. The highly ambitious fourth plan was never adopted by the government, and even within the Planning Board, it failed to receive universal support. In the same year, a group of planners within the Planning Board, together with specialists from ILPES, produced a study entitled 'Bases for a development strategy in the context of Andean integration' (JNPC, 1969c) as a preliminary document for the preparation of a fifth plan. This study placed greater emphasis upon Ecuador's social, agrarian and regional development problems than the 1970–1973 plan, but, again, it was effectively ignored by the government (see Moncada, 1973b, 27–8).

Ecuador's fifth national plan, entitled 'Integral plan of transformation and development 1973–77' (JNPC, 1972) was prepared in 1971–72 to cover the country's first five years as a major oil exporter. Because it is the most recent plan, and the one which was still operative at the time of writing of this monograph, it merits more detailed attention than the earlier national plans. The fifth plan followed the pattern of the first four national plans in its concentration upon economic planning by sectors and its lack of specific directives to facilitate effective implementation. Relatively little attention was given to social affairs or to the regional distribution of development, and emphasis was put upon rapid economic growth. The plan assumed an average annual growth in gdp of 10.1% and an average

82

TABLE 12

GOVERNMENT INVESTMENT SPECIFIED IN THE FOURTH NATIONAL
PLAN, 1970–1973

Expressed as percentages of the total four-year expenditure

Calculated from data in JNPC (1969b, I, 400).

	Government Investment %
Agriculture, fisheries and forestry ...	13.5
Irrigation	9.5
Industry	2.4
Electrification	14.0
Transport and telecommunications	37.1
Education	9.1
Health	3.4
Regional development	3.1
Others	7.9
TOTAL (%)	100.0

annual growth in exports of 16.4% between 1973 and 1977. It assumed a massive increase in government revenues and expenditures due to the development of oil exports, and a continued inflow of foreign investment capital and development aid. Investment targets were presented in much greater detail than in previous plans, and the planned distribution of government and private investment is given in Table 13. 40% of total planned investment was expected to come from national and local government bodies, and the remaining 60% was expected to come from private enterprise. Planning for the private sector was indicative in character, providing incentives to attract investment in particular fields, but not adopting mandatory measures to force private enterprise to comply with the plan's targets. Compared with the previous national plans, increased emphasis was given to petroleum, industrialization, fisheries, transport, tele-communications and tourism. Major investment was continued in irrigation and electrification, but relatively, though not absolutely, the amount of investment given to agriculture, social services and housing was reduced.

83

TABLE 13

GOVERNMENT AND PRIVATE INVESTMENT SPECIFIED IN THE FIFTH
NATIONAL PLAN, 1973–1977

Expressed as percentages of the total five-year expenditure

Calculated from data in JNPC (1972, 14).

	Government Investment %	Private Investment %	Total Investment %
Agriculture and livestock	2.4	14.3	9.5
Fisheries	2.4	0.5	1.3
Forestry	1.4	0.2	0.7
Agrarian reform	1.7	5.4	3.9
Colonization	0.6	0.6	0.6
Irrigation	5.0	0.2	2.1
Hydrocarbons (mainly oil) and mining ...	1.7	18.7	11.8
Industry and artisan production	11.1	23.4	18.5
Construction	0.0	3.0	1.8
Electrification	18.0	1.9	8.4
Roads	20.6	0.0	8.3
Railways, ports and airports	4.5	0.0	1.8
Motor vehicles, ships and aircraft	3.1	11.9	8.3
Post and telecommunications	4.6	0.0	1.9
Education	4.9	1.1	2.6
Urban development and housing	3.7	15.0	10.5
Health	5.1	0.2	2.2
Water supply and sewerage	6.8	0.0	2.7
Services and commerce	0.0	3.2	1.9
Public administration	1.7	0.0	0.7
Tourism	0.4	0.4	0.4
Others (rural development, cooperatives, meteorology, hydrology, social welfare and vocational training)	0.3	0.0	0.1
TOTAL (%)	100.0	100.0	100.0
Total five-year expenditure in millions of sucres at 1972 prices	31,750.0	47,178.9	78,928.9

The fifth national plan contemplated a considerable extension
of the activities of central government into manufacturing, electricity
generation, local road construction and agricultural marketing,
fields which have traditionally been managed by private enterprise
and by local government. The ambitious growth and investment
targets were linked to manpower policies intended to reduce the

84

current levels of unemployment and underemployment, and it was expected that most subsistence farmers would be absorbed into the national economy within the five-year plan period. As well as the traditional ideas of import-substitution industrialization proposed in Ecuador's first four national plans, but never fully implemented, a new emphasis was placed upon the development of exports of manufactured goods and the reduction of dependence upon a few major trading partners. The social goals of the plan were far from ambitious. Although there was a considerable amount of egalitarian rhetoric, discussing the integration of the 'marginal population' into the labour force and the implementation of programmes of agrarian reform and 'social mobilization', there was little definite indication of specific programmes which were likely to assist the poorest sections of the population. The increased wealth and inflation associated with the oil boom has served to accentuate the socio-economic disparities between regions and social classes, and the plan proposed little to counteract these trends.

The 'Integral plan of transformation and development 1973–77', was written in the months immediately following the accession to power of Rodríguez Lara's 'Revolutionary Nationalist Government', and remained the Ecuadorian government's basic policy document even after the resignation of Rodríguez Lara in January 1976. In many senses, the plan was a direct successor to the initial policy statements of the 'Revolutionary Nationalist Government' (GRNE, 1972), combining wild promises of social and economic transformations, and of the ending of dependency, with great imprecision regarding the actual measures to be adopted. The plan was mainly written by the most leftist and idealistic members of the Planning Board, who saw it as a means of leading the government towards radical reforms. As with most Ecuadorian government documents proposing radical changes, the details of these changes were rarely specified. To some extent, the lack of specification of details reflected the caution of a good poker player, who postpones revealing his hand until the last moment, so as to make sure that his opponents cannot effectively oppose his strategy. To a greater extent, however, the vague nature of the plan reflected a lack of commitment and of detailed planning on the part of the government, as well as a desire to avoid arousing opposition within and outside the regime. The plan was essentially a continuation of the Ecuadorian populist tradition, combining revolutionary rhetoric appealing to leftist intellectuals, and to the lower classes, with imprecision and inactivity, so as not to arouse the hostility of national and foreign elites. To the more left-wing members of the 'Revolutionary Nationalist Government', the 'Philosophy and plan of action of the Government' (GRNE, 1972), and the 'Integral plan of transformation and development' were the great declarations of intent of the regime, symbolizing the actions which would earn popular adulation and lasting power for the government. To the more right-wing members, however, the documents were simply typical government documents, published to appease particular interest groups, but not intended for effective implementation. As the 'Revolutionary Nationalist Government' drifted towards the political right during Rodríguez Lara's Presidency, and as all of the major promised reforms became bogged down in bureaucracy and official apathy, the right-wing view of the regime's early publications proved to be correct.

The idealism and impracticality of the 'Integral plan of transformation and development' is well indicated by the letter of presentation at the beginning of the plan (JNPC, 1972, v), signed by the President of the Board:

'. . . I would like to emphasize . . . that for the first time in the history of the country, all of the organizations responsible for the execution of the plan and all of the regions of the country have participated in the elaboration of this document. . . . The process of planning demands the joint effort of the people and of the government of Ecuador, in a perspective of permanent integration and solidarity in the search for very well-defined objectives to consolidate our economic independence and humanistic social development. The concept which inspired the preparation of the document was that of creating equal opportunities for all Ecuadorians, as the only way to guarantee national unity and to achieve development. This document contains historic decisions intended to increase production and to improve the situation of all Ecuadorians . . .'

Even Velasco Ibarra could not have written a more impressive, imprecise and impractical set of statements and proposals ! The document was meant to impress everyone, and to displease no-one, with preambles and summaries following closely in the traditions of Ecuadorian populism. It served admirably as a publicity document and status symbol for a new regime, and it matched the 'oil bonanza'

86

mentality which has pervaded Ecuador since 1970. In Rodríguez Lara's own words, development would be achieved by 'sowing petroleum', investing oil revenues in infrastructure, agriculture and industrial production. There was little call for saving, austerity, or sacrifice, and no implication that any section of the population would be disadvantaged by the changes implied in the plan. Instead, the tone of the plan was one of universal participation in the bountiful wealth afforded by oil.

Within a few months of its publication, the 'Integral plan of transformation and development' became increasingly irrelevant as government oil revenues grew with the massive rises in world oil prices and the increasing government participation in those prices which followed the Arab-Israeli war in 1973, and the quadrupling of government oil revenues within a year and a half. The plan was based on an estimated oil production of 400,000 barrels per day in 1977, whilst only about half that total is now thought to be a realistic production target. Thus, for the latter half of the plan period, Ecuador is now expected to export about half as much oil as planned, but to obtain revenues on each barrel of oil about four times higher than those projected in the plan. These massive changes in the whole basis of Ecuador's economy, reflect Ecuador's dependency upon fluctuations in the world economy which are essentially outside Ecuadorian control. Given the great increases in oil revenues after the completion of the plan, it is not surprising that the President of the Board was able to announce in 1975 that all of the sectors of the Ecuadorian economy except agriculture had exceeded their planned production targets (*El Tiempo*, 7 agosto 1975, p 1). These achievements were claimed as credits to the National Planning Board, but in reality, they are simply reflections of Ecuador's fortunes in the world market for primary products. Good fortune in international trade can generate a period of economic growth, high investment and rapid consumption, whether or not a plan document states that this should take place. It is already clear that the 'Integral plan of transformation and development' has failed to achieve the total transformation of Ecuador's economy and society necessary to achieve the most important objectives embodied in the plan (JNPC, 1972, 4):

'1. To achieve an integral strengthening of the country, through the achievement of a greater degree of national integration and a constant reaffirmation of Ecuadorian sovereignty.

87

2. To improve the living conditions of the Ecuadorian citizen, and especially those of the groups who today are immersed in the most abject poverty, and who include large sections of society.

3. To stimulate and expand the country's productive potential, through a better use of natural resources and a more rational utilization of the territory, changes which will permit a growth in the capacity of the system to absorb labour in the increasing levels of production'.

Although these 'ends' of the plan have not been achieved, and are unlikely to be achieved in the foreseeable future, many of the 'means' specified in the plan have now become reality, the two most significant examples being the growth in government participation in most facets of the economy and the rapid expansion of light industries assisted by foreign capital and technology. It is clear, however, that, like the achievement of most of the sectoral production targets of the plan, these changes are almost inevitable concomitants of the rapid inflow of foreign exchange and the growth of government revenues in Ecuador. The fact that they were included in the plan does not indicate that they were effectively 'planned' by the National Planning Board.

Sectoral planning

Since the early 1950s, a considerable number of specialized plans have been prepared for specific aspects of the Ecuadorian economy, both by national government bodies and by firms of foreign consultants. For reasons of space, it is only possible in this monograph to list some of the most important plans in each sector of the economy.

In the field of agriculture, there have been two major plans. The first, by Italconsult (1963), provided a great deal of useful information, but, like most studies on Ecuador produced by foreign companies, it erred heavily on the side of excessive optimism about the potential for rapid development. The second, by the National Planning Board (JNPC, 1964a), was more realistic but, like the Italconsult plan, it gave insufficient emphasis to agrarian reform as a precondition for major agricultural development.

Artisan production and small-scale industry were the subjects of a special plan by the National Planning Board (JNPC, 1969a) for the period 1969–1973, giving a detailed framework for rapid expansion under the auspices of various national and regional development organizations. In the field of industrial development, almost two hundred special studies have been produced by the Industrial Development Centre (CENDES), an organization set up in 1961 to promote industrialization. Each of the special studies puts forward a scheme for the establishment of a particular industry in the hope that the idea will be adopted by private enterprise. The industries proposed range from such obvious cases as fertilizers, bricks and nylon to unusual possibilities like yucca starch and dried garlic. CENDES has also made detailed evaluations of Latin American markets for Ecuadorian products, and a number of plans for export promotion of specific products have been prepared. A more general study of the possibilities of increasing Ecuador's exports has been prepared by the Surveys and Research Corporation (Watkins, 1967), and C R Gibson (1971) has examined the structure of Ecuador's foreign trade, evaluating alternative development strategies and possible changes in the system of tariffs, licences and export incentives.

In the case of public works, the main specialized national plans have been for transportation. The most important ones have been the four national road plans prepared by the Ministry of Public Works (MOP, 1953, 1964, 1969 and 1973), and the 1964 National Transportation Plan (PBQD, 1964). In addition, various plans have been prepared for the improvement of the national railway system (*eg* EFE, 1958).

Apart from transport, the most important national public works plans have been the National Sanitation Plan (SCISP, 1961), which presented detailed water supply and sewerage projects for every parish centre in the country, and the National Electrification Plans (JNPC, 1956a; and INECEL, 1971) which outlined the construction of a national grid system and specified an order of development for major power projects.

The first major sectoral approach to the planning of social services on a national scale was the National Education Plan produced by the Ministry of Education (MEP, 1964). This was prepared in coordination with the third integral national plan of the National Planning Board, and concentrated mainly on primary and secondary education, with brief sections on higher and adult education schemes. In the same year, the Stanford Research Institute prepared a study of manpower and educational needs in Ecuador (McCusker and Podesta, 1964) concentrating particularly upon higher education and professional and technical training. The Stanford study eventually led in 1970 to the publication of a national plan for human resources prepared by the National Planning Board in conjunction with Ohio State University and the Organization of American States. This plan recommended targets for a major and relatively balanced expansion in all levels of education. Insufficient attention was given, however, to the quality and type of education necessary, the optimum spatial distribution of educational facilities, and the special educational requirements of the most underprivileged sections of the population.

In general, the numerous sectoral plans prepared in Ecuador have suffered the same fate as the integral national plans; a limited and relatively ineffective degree of implementation, and then a gradual passage into oblivion. The sectoral plans have brought considerable prestige to the institutions that prepared them or commissioned their preparation, but they have not brought the benefits of planned development to Ecuador. Indeed, the sectoral plans have frequently actually impeded planned development by diverting attention away from the integral national plans, and by creating an atmosphere of confusion. Thus, in 1972, for example, North American and Ecuadorian consultants were engaged in preparing the fourth national road plan for the Ministry of Public Works at the same time as the fifth integral national plan was being prepared by the National Planning Board. Naturally, the Board's integral national plan included road-building targets and priorities, yet these targets and priorities were only loosely related to the Ministry of Public Works' targets and priorities. The simultaneous preparation of the two plans led to duplication in data collection and analysis, and to the publication of two contradictory documents, yet neither plan has been effectively implemented. Some planned roads have never even been initiated, whilst other roads have been initiated, and occasionally even completed, even though they do not appear in either plan. The percentage of the Ministry of Public Works' national road plans which has been implemented is probably higher than the corresponding levels of implementation for any other government sectoral plans, but even for roads, the efforts and resources expended in planning are at least half wasted.

90

FIGURE 6: MAJOR REGIONAL AND LOCAL DEVELOPMENT PROJECTS

Regional planning

The actual and optimum distributions of economic activity have been given remarkably little attention in most of Ecuador's national development plans. The relatively high centralization of government in Quito has generally inhibited planning on a regional or sub-regional scale. The regional plans that have been prepared can be divided into four basic types: provincial and multi-provincial development plans; integrated river-basin development plans; colonization and road plans for the eastern lowlands and the northern coastal lowlands; and the special plans for frontier integration with Colombia and Peru.

Provincial and multi-provincial development planning began in the mid-1950s with the publication of a special study of Azuay and Cañar provinces by the National Planning Board (JNPC, 1956b) and the establishment of CREA[23] in 1958 to stimulate development in Azuay, Cañar and Morona-Santiago provinces. Azuay and Cañar had entered a period of depression in the fifties due to the decline of their traditional artisan production of Panama hats, mounting rural population pressure, and a series of poor harvests. CREA was designated to cover Morona-Santiago as well as Azuay and Cañar, so as to include the whole of the town of Cuenca's effective area of influence and to link highland development with pioneer colonization in the eastern lowlands. CREA has worked in the fields of agricultural extension, irrigation, colonization, community development, electrification, artisan production and industrialization, and it has produced various regional development projects in collaboration with the Inter-American Development Bank (see IADB, 1963; CREA, 1970). Most of CREA's work has been in the preparation and execution of small-scale projects in a wide range of different fields. As a regional development organization, CREA has given relatively little attention to long-range, or large-scale planning. CREA's approach has been highly pragmatic, and CREA has achieved much more in the field of project implementation than any other regional development organization in Ecuador. CREA has functioned as a relatively effective 'pressure group', attracting national government assistance to the Cuenca area. For many years, industrial development in Azuay and Cañar was greatly assisted by a special law, dating from 1954, giving new industries in the two provinces a decade's operation

---

23 *Centro de Reconversión Económica del Azuay, Cañar y Morona-Santiago.*

92

without payment of taxes. In CREA's early years, the organization succeeded in attracting a substantial number of new industries to Cuenca, reinforcing Cuenca's position as Ecuador's third urban centre, and generating some new employment in the Cuenca zone. CREA has always been based in Cuenca and staffed mainly by local personnel, giving the organization strong local support and a considerable institutional separation from the national government. Three major criticisms can be levelled at CREA. First, the inhabitants of Cañar province can claim, with some justification, that CREA has tended to favour Azuay in the location of its projects. Secondly, many CREA projects, and particularly the earlier ones, had no pre-project feasibility studies, causing numerous failures and frequent duplication of CREA's efforts. Thirdly, many of CREA's projects are of the type normally undertaken by national government Ministries, or by provincial councils and cantonal authorities. The result has been further duplication and increased inter-institutional rivalries.

Following the relatively successful example of CREA, three further multi-provincial development authorities were set up in the sixties: CORFODEC,[24] for the provinces of Chimborazo, Bolívar and Los Rios; CORFONOR,[25] for the provinces of Esmeraldas, Carchi, Imbabura and Napo; and the Development Board for the provinces of Loja and Zamora-Chinchipe. These authorities achieved very little before they were abolished in 1970 by a special decree of President Velasco Ibarra, so that now only CREA remains a multi-provincial development authority. CORFODEC, CORFONOR and the Development Board for Loja and Zamora-Chinchipe represent an interesting, if rather short-lived, attempt to decentralize develop-ment planning and to introduce a practical application of the idea of 'geo-economic belts', west-east zones showing a functional integration through labour migration and the exchange of products between contrasting ecological areas (see Oquendo, 1968; and 1971, 1–7). This principle of functional west-east integration contrasts strongly with the traditional, formal division of Ecuador into relatively uniform natural regions running north-south. During the sixties, Manabí, Guayas, El Oro and Tungurahua, provinces which were not involved in the multi-provincial development authorities, established their own local, single-province development authorities linked to the provincial

24 *Corporación de Fomento del Centro de la República.*
25 *Corporación de Fomento del Norte.*

councils, and some of the provinces formerly in multi-provincial authorities have now followed their lead. In most of these provinces, however, the provincial development authorities have been too small-scale and too poorly-financed to make any significant contribution. At best, they have served as discussion forums, pressing the provincial councils and cantonal authorities to undertake specific projects, and expressing provincial interests to sections of the national government. At worst, they have merely further overloaded an existing complex administrative structure, wasting finance on salaries and office rents.

Two provincial development authorities stand out from the rest as larger and more successful organizations: the Integrated Office for the Planning of Esmeraldas (OIPE),[26] and the Centre for the Rehabilitation of Manabí (CRM).[27] The OIPE was established in 1974 by the provincial council of Esmeraldas and the municipality of the town of Esmeraldas, with technical assistance from the Organization of American States. It has been involved in the preparation of provincial resource assessments and development projects and has prepared an urban development plan for the town of Esmeraldas. The CRM was established in 1962 after a serious drought in southern and central Manabí, and it has developed into a sizeable organization involved in both regional planning and plan implementation. CRM has concentrated upon water resource development, and particularly the Poza Honda scheme in central Manabí (see Agrar und Hydrotechnic GMBH, 1972). In addition to Poza Honda, one of the largest irrigation schemes in Ecuador, CRM has prepared, and is in the course of constructing, a wide variety of smaller irrigation and water supply projects. CRM has also done a considerable amount of agricultural extension work, and like CREA, it is attached to the Ecuadorian Ministry of Agriculture.

In response to vociferous local protests that the province of Carchi has been neglected by the national government, the National Planning Board produced a special development plan for the province in 1962 (JNPC, 1962), but political changes subsequently prevented the plan's implementation. A similar plan was produced by the Board in 1971 for the reconstruction and development of the drought- and earthquake-stricken province of Loja (JNPC, 1971), concentrating

---

[26] *Oficina Integrada de Planificación de Esmeraldas.*
[27] *Centre de Rehabilitación de Manabí.*

on measures to improve the living standards and education of the 'marginal population' living in remote rural areas. Since the preparation of the special plans for Carchi and Loja, the National Planning Board has prepared a succession of further provincial studies and plans (eg JNPC, 1973b, 1974). These efforts by the Board have been token responses to provincial pressures upon the national government. The whole procedure has been simply a mechanism for defusing tension. The provincial plans are far too vague to be implemented, and there is little or no administrative will or institutional coordination to ensure their implementation. Local initiatives by individual governors and provincial councils have also sometimes led to the preparation of provincial development plans by provincial authorities (eg CPEO, 1973; GMM and CPM, 1975), but in reality, these plans have been little more than unsuccessful appeals for funds from the national government.

In 1963, an Organization of American States research team made an integrated natural resource evaluation of the Guayas river basin in the coastal lowlands (PAU, 1964), and this pioneer study has grown into the most important regional development programme in Ecuador. The aim has been to combine physical, environmental and agricultural studies with socio-economic research in order to produce a detailed plan for regional development based mainly on an intensive utilization of the basin's water resources. The main development plans for the Guayas basin were published in 1970 (Ingledow and Associates, 1970), providing detailed natural resource data, brief social and economic studies and preliminary plans for three major civil engineering projects: a hydroelectric scheme in the Chimbo valley of Bolívar province; an irrigation scheme around Babahoyo in Los Rios province; and a combined hydroelectric and irrigation scheme in the Daule–Peripa area of Guayas province. Since the publication of the main development plans, the area officially covered by the Guayas basin programme has been extended to include the Santa Elena peninsula to the west, an area which is undergoing an economic depression due to the gradual exhaustion of its oilfields, which have been continuously exploited since the early decades of this century. In practice, however, since 1970, the Guayas basin programme has almost abandoned the principle of broad, integrated regional planning and has concentrated upon the detailed planning of the Babahoyo and Daule–Peripa projects.

95

The regional development authority which has charge of the Guayas basin programme is known as CEDEGE,[28] and is based in Guayaquil. Since its establishment in 1965, CEDEGE has gradually reduced its dependence upon foreign technicians, and has built up a substantial local staff. It has come to be identified with the interests and aspirations of the Guayaquil elites, and has adopted a markedly technocratic approach to its work. In general, CEDEGE is only concerned with the provinces of Guayas and Los Rios, even though its notional 'territory' includes parts of eight Ecuadorian provinces. CEDEGE has shown little interest in small projects, or in short-term projects. For over a decade, it has been immersed in detailed feasibility studies for large-scale engineering projects in the field of water resource development. CEDEGE's grandiose projects have been good news for Guayaquil's construction contractors, industrialists and land speculators, and there has been surprisingly little concern about the failure of CEDEGE to consider smaller-scale schemes which are potentially more labour intensive and cost-effective. The case of CEDEGE illustrates a general tendency in Ecuadorian development to concentrate attention upon very large-scale, long-term engineering projects, which depend heavily upon foreign finance, technical expertise and technology. This phenomenon is not just the fault of local 'racketeers' and speculators, and of over-ambitious politicians. It is also the fault of foreign consultants and contractors, and of foreign aid 'donors', all of whom stand to gain most from this type of project. 'Aid' is big business, and since 1963, there has been an undignified scramble by foreign-interest groups to become involved in the Guayas basin programme, a scramble which has completely distorted the original objectives of balanced, integral regional development.

As a result of the publicity attached to the Guayas basin programme, and of the pressure for integrated river basin development from the Organization of American States and other international bodies, four further river basin development programmes have been initiated in Ecuador. The two most important, the Puyango-Tumbes and Catamayo-Chira programmes on the Ecuadorian-Peruvian border, will be discussed later in the context of frontier integration. Just to the north of those programmes, the provincial council of El Oro province has initiated studies for the integral development of the

<hr>

28 *Comisión de Estudios para el Desarrollo de la Cuenca del Río Guayas.*

basin of the River Jubones, covering parts of the provinces of El Oro, Loja and Azuay. The first major consultants' report (Halcrow and Partners, 1971) has led to detailed feasibility studies for a variety of hydroelectric power generation, irrigation and flood-control projects. In northern Ecuador, studies have been initiated for the integral development of the basins of the Rivers Esmeraldas and Santiago, covering sections of the provinces of Esmeraldas, Manabí, Pichincha, Imbabura and Cotopaxi. These studies are administered by a Commission for the Development of the Esmeraldas and Santiago Basins, based in Quito, and strongly assisted by the Organization of American States.

A number of combined road and colonization plans for the eastern lowlands were produced by the National Colonization Institute (INC, 1961, 1962a and 1962b) before the Institute was incorporated in 1964 into the newly created Ecuadorian Institute for Agrarian Reform and Colonization (IERAC). These plans were never implemented, but three subsequent, more specialized plans for the eastern lowlands have been at least partially implemented: the marginal highway plan for a north-south road running along the eastern fringes of the Andes and connecting the main colonization zones in the Oriente (see TAMS, 1965; Bromley, 1972, 282); the special road and colonization plans for Morona-Santiago province prepared by CREA (*eg* 1970); and the road construction plans for Napo province prepared by the Ecuadorian section of the Brazilian-Ecuadorian Integration Commission (CMEB, 1970). Similar transport and colonization plans were prepared in the 1950s for the northern part of Esmeraldas province by the Quito-San Lorenzo Autonomous Railroad Board[29] (see Acosta-Solís, 1959, 105–27; Whitten, 1965, 28–32). It should be emphasized, however, that none of the regional colonization plans prepared in Ecuador have been even one-tenth implemented. The majority of the limited developments which have occurred in the areas concerned have been due to spontaneous settlement by individual families and to the road-building efforts of foreign companies seeking to discover or exploit local resources.

In 1966, the Inter-American Development Bank produced a plan for the economic development and integration of the frontier provinces on both sides of the Ecuadorian-Colombian border, concentrating particularly upon a coordinated public works programme (IADB,

---

29 *Junta Autónoma del Ferrocarril Quito-San Lorenzo.*

97

1966). This plan has been formally adopted by the Ecuadorian and Colombia governments, but to date, there has been little progress in its implementation. The Inter-American Development Bank's initiative followed the establishment of an Ecuadorian-Colombian Integration Commission[30] in 1962, and led to the establishment in 1967 of a regional development office in Tulcan known as the Secretariat for Ecuadorian-Colombian Frontier Integration (SIFCE-DE).[31] SIFCE-DE was attached to the Ecuadorian Ministry of Industry, Commerce and Integration, and was finally converted into a regional office of the Ministry in 1974. In spite of so many administrative changes, the regional development office in Tulcan has never had any significant effect upon the development of northern Ecuador, or upon frontier integration with Colombia. It has been continuously starved of resources and has failed to coordinate effectively with other organizations in Northern Ecuador.

Northern Ecuador is one of the areas of the country which best illustrates the failure to achieve an integral form of regional development. Vast areas of Esmeraldas and Napo provinces have no roads, railways or air services, though many of these areas are suitable for colonization. The provinces of Carchi and Imbabura have no direct links except mule trails to the eastern lowlands, and they have only one link, the antiquated Ibarra–San Lorenzo Railway, to the northern coastal lowlands. Remarkably little political pressure has been generated to integrate the different sections of northern Ecuador with one another. Efforts have been dissipated in a wide variety of small, ineffectual projects, a wastage of resources resulting mainly from the intense rivalry of different towns and ports, and from the total lack of integrated planning. The Ecuadorian government has deliberately avoided implementing projects for the regional integration of northern Ecuador, so contradicting the objectives it has stated in numerous plans and in the various integration discussions with Colombia. Three major factors have influenced the Ecuadorian government in taking this very negative attitude. First, there has long been a deep-rooted fear of Colombian commercial and industrial penetration in Ecuador. As a result, little effort has been made to develop the frontier areas, or to establish new cross-border links, so as to limit

---

30 *Comisión Permanente de Integración Económica Ecuatoriara-Colombiana.*
31 *Secretaría de Integración Fronteriza Ecuatoriana-Colombiana, División del Ecuador* (SIFCE-DE).

such potential penetration. Second, the mercantile interests of Quito have tended to resist measures which would enable Esmeraldas, Ibarra and Tulcan to extend their areas of influence, and to establish strong west-east communication links. The effective development of northern Ecuador as a functional region has been mistakenly considered as a threat to Quito's primacy over the northern half of the country. In fact, the negative attitude of Ecuador's Quito-based central government has actually weakened Quito's position *vis-à-vis* Guayaquil, whose commercial interests have always opposed the development of north-western Ecuador. Third, the interest-groups associated with the antiquated and badly maintained San Lorenzo Railway, have opposed the construction of alternative communications links which might deprive the railway of the pathetically small volume of traffic that it actually carries. Even more than other regions of Ecuador, northern Ecuador's development has been impeded by local rivalries and short-sighted, self-centred thinking, problems which are almost insurmountable obstacles to effective planning.

The idea of frontier integration between Ecuador and Peru is much more controversial than between Ecuador and Colombia because of Ecuador's long-standing territorial disputes with Peru. In spite of this, the situation has recently improved for two main reasons: pressure from international organizations; and the improvement in Ecuadorian-Peruvian relations resulting from Andean Integration and from the Ecuadorian government's recent policy of not pressing its territorial claims too strongly for fear of endangering its north-eastern oilfields. In 1971, an Ecuadorian-Peruvian Economic Commission[32] was established, and this led to the signing of a treaty for the joint use of two river basins which are each divided by the frontier, the Catamayo-Chira basin, and the Puyango-Tumbes basin (see JNPC, 1975a, 54–55). The two countries then established a Commission for the Development of the Puyango-Tumbes and Catamayo-Chira Basins,[33] the Commission being divided into two national Subcommissions. The Ecuadorian Subcommission, usually known as PREDESUR,[34] has grown rapidly as a river basin development authority, and as a regional development authority for the

---

[32] *Comisión Económica Permanente Ecuatoriana-Peruana.*
[33] *Comisión Mixta Ecuatoriana-Peruana para el Aprovechamiento de las Cuencas Hidrográficas Binacionales Puyango-Tumbes y Catamayo-Chira.*
[34] *Programa Regional para el Desarrollo de la Región Sur del Ecuador.*

frontier provinces of El Oro, Loja and Zamora-Chinchipe. Since PREDESUR began work in 1971, it has been the most innovative and rapidly-growing regional development authority in Ecuador. It has undertaken detailed water resource studies, and has begun small projects in the fields of agriculture, forestry and settlement (see *eg* PREDESUR, 1974 and 1975). Much of its area of operation in the provinces of Loja and El Oro is semi-arid, and particular emphasis has been given to the design of irrigation schemes. PREDESUR has generally avoided the use of foreign consultants and has gathered together a strong team of Ecuadorian engineers. It has been relatively successful in coordinating with other government departments, and with provincial and cantonal authorities, and has avoided the adverse criticism which has so often affected CEDEGE. PREDESUR has adopted a most peculiar, though very pragmatic, system of operation. It maintains its head office in Quito, with local offices in various towns in El Oro and Loja provinces. This system of working enables the senior staff of PREDESUR to maintain close contact with the Ecuadorian government, and it may well be the best adaptation to the distribution of power in Ecuador. The system is liable to criticism, however, because of the high cost of travel, communication and expenses payments for staff moving between Quito, Machala and Loja and because of the unfamiliarity of many of the staff with the areas that they are actually planning.

The overall picture presented by regional planning in Ecuador is one of instability and confusion. A considerable variety of past authorities no longer exist and many of the present authorities are unlikely to last long in their present form. Each authority developed at a different time, for a different reason, with a different system of finance and different patterns of operation. Some of the authorities overlap in territory, while many parts of the country are covered by no regional authority (see JNPC, 1975b). The linkages between the regional development authorities and the national government vary enormously from one authority to another. Some of the provincial authorities have no effective linkage to the national government, having simply grown out of provincial and cantonal initiatives. The result of this institutional confusion is that the objectives and plans of the regional authorities bear little relation to the objectives and plans of the national government, and there is a tendency for the regional authorities to initiate more projects than the nation can

100

support. This latter problem is particularly important in the field of water resource development, where the many projects prepared by CRM, CEDEGE, CREA, PREDESUR, etc frequently overlap with, or compete for scarce funds with, the projects of INECEL, the national electrification authority, and INERHI, the national irrigation authority.

The necessity to coordinate regional development authorities within a national/regional planning framework, and to link regional objectives to national objectives has been widely recognized, and some progress has been made recently towards this end (eg JNPC, 1975a, 1975b and 1975c). Many would argue, however, that the creation of a well-organized regional planning system in Ecuador, and the effective coordination of municipal, provincial, regional and national authorities, will simply strengthen the power of the national government. It will not lead to any devolution of power to the regional and local levels, or to any effective system of popular participation in decision making. As a result, though the establishment of an effective regional planning system will certainly improve the efficiency of government, it will probably not lead to the reduction of regional inequalities or to local social mobilization and the proliferation of self-help projects.

Local planning

The majority of local plans produced in Ecuador have been for civil engineering schemes and urban development. Detailed studies have been produced for a large number of hydroelectric, irrigation and road construction projects in different parts of the country, and special plans have been drawn up for the creation of deep-water ports on the Pacific coast and for the improvement of the airports at Guayaquil and Quito. Most of the provincial capitals and several cantonal capitals have prepared their own plans for future urban growth,[35] but few have subsequently followed the plans, so that urban expansion has continued to be haphazard. The legal constraints on private building are insufficient to allow a town or city government fully to control urban development, and plan implementation has often been limited to the control of urban land invasions and the enforcement of building lines along major road axes.

[35] Such a plan is generally called a *plan regulador*.

Detailed local colonization plans have been prepared for various areas in the eastern lowlands and in the northern coastal lowlands (eg CREA, 1970; IERAC, 1965, 1966, 1970a and 1970b). Of these plans, however, none has been more than partially implemented, and many have not been implemented at all. Until recently, there were no detailed local social and economic development plans for the settled rural areas of Ecuador. However, since 1970, some progress has been made, initially through the work of the Andean Mission (MAE, 1970a and 1970b), and subsequently, after the amalgamation of the Andean Mission with the Ministry of Agriculture, by the Ministry in collaboration with the Inter-American Development Bank (see IADB, 1973). As yet, however, such welcome initiatives have not led to any effective action in the field of integrated rural development.

At the local level, as at the regional and national levels, there has been a strong tendency on the part of government to plan in a technocratic and almost dictatorial fashion. There has been no established system of local consultation, or of popular participation in the planning process, and widespread apathy towards government plans and projects has been the inevitable result. Even the suggestion of participation in planning has been considered as 'heresy' by some government officials. In one case, a United Nations expert who initiated a survey of local aspirations in the provinces of Imbabura and Esmeraldas was given 24 hours to leave the country. The resistance of Ecuadorian authorities at all levels to any form of effective participation or community development, is, of course, hidden by a 'democratic mask'; the statement in almost all plans that the proposals have resulted from widespread consultation, and will be for the common good. In reality, consultations are usually limited to discussions with local elites, and development plans reflect the techno-cratic leanings and foreign dependence of the planners, politicians and other elite groups involved. As a result, there is no widespread commitment to the achievement of planned objectives, and plans are usually made obsolete by any change of government. 'Development' is usually viewed as something which is handed down from above, rather than generated from below, reflecting the persistence of paternalism at all levels of Ecuadorian government, and the marginali-zation of the majority of Ecuador's population from any participation in decision making.

CHAPTER V

Conclusion

'. . . enormous growth in primary commodities produced by foreign concessions for export has been unaccompanied either by structural changes to induce complementary growth or by institutional changes to diffuse gains in real income among all sectors of the population. Our principal conclusion is that the rapid growth in production . . . has had little developmental impact . . . It has increased the wage bill for unskilled labour and has expanded tax revenues received by the government. But the enlarged wage bill has not induced expansion of domestic production of goods bought by wage workers; it has merely raised imports. And increased tax revenues have been spent for the most part in ways that do not appreciably increase the productive capacity of the nation . . .' (Clower, Dalton, Harwitz and Walters, 1966, vi).

THIS QUOTATION FROM the classic work on Liberia entitled 'Growth without Development' mirrors the hollowness of much of Ecuador's recent economic growth and reflects the weaknesses of dependent development. Since 1972, Ecuador has gone through one of the most significant periods of economic growth in her history, yet, so far, this growth has brought little benefit to the average Ecuadorian. The development which has occurred has mainly been 'incrementalist' rather than 'transformationalist', continuing and accentuating past trends, rather than achieving radical changes in the social and economic structure. Unearned windfalls rarely bring great happiness, and Ecuador's oil wealth is no exception to this rule. The economic crisis of 1975 and the fall of Rodríguez Lara at the beginning of 1976, both indicate the hollowness of the oil boom and the failure effectively to 'sow oil' to encourage long-term economic security and growth. The Ecuadorian government has become vulnerable to the pressures of major international oil companies and oil-consuming countries. In addition, the Ecuadorian economy has probably become more susceptible than ever before to natural disasters, as landslides and floods often cause temporary breaks in the Trans-Andean oil pipeline and the cessation of exports. A few weeks without the nourishment of oil revenues can turn Ecuador's economy from prosperity to bankruptcy, and can weaken or even topple the

national government. Ecuador's dependence upon foreign investment, technology and expertise, and above all, upon foreign export
markets, has been accentuated by the oil bonanza, making the country
even more vulnerable to the pressures of foreign interest groups.

Of course, Ecuador has greater prospects of real development with
oil than without it, but so far, the appropriate steps have not been
taken to bring about positive changes in the socio-economic system.
The author feels that three major changes are required to bring about
a transformation of the Ecuadorian economy and society, and to set
Ecuador upon the road towards social justice and improvements in
the living standards of the majority of the population. First, and
foremost, there should be a large-scale redistribution of income and
wealth in Ecuadorian society, enabling the enormous lower class to
participate more effectively in production and consumption.[36] This
would require: a new, sweeping land reform; a clamp-down on luxury
consumption; a narrowing of wage differentials; an increase in
taxation of upper-class groups; the development of a system of
incentives and savings schemes to encourage national investment;
a major reorientation of investment away from Quito and Guayaquil;
a concentration of infrastructural and social investments in rural
areas and urban slums; and a large-scale programme to encourage
the growth of small, Ecuadorian-owned businesses in all sectors of
the economy. Such measures would greatly increase the potential
for long-term growth in production, and for the development of a mass
market for Ecuadorian products.

Secondly, there should be an emphasis upon social mobilization,
popular participation and self-management.[37] This would require:
the introduction of universal adult suffrage; the elimination of
paternalism from government activities; the encouragement of effective
cooperatives; and the promotion of self-help projects to solve the
most pressing problems of poor neighbourhoods. Throughout her
history, Ecuador's most fundamental problem has been the underutilization of her own resources (see Bottomley, 1966; Salz, 1955),
the most important underutilized resource of all being her own population. Mass poverty combined with upper-class and government

---

[36] The need for a redistribution of income and wealth in Ecuador is recognized
by several prominent Ecuadorian economists who have worked in the government
(eg Moncada, 1973a; Santos, 1975, 19–33).

[37] For explanations of mobilization, participation and self-management, see
Friedmann (1973) and Vanek (1975).

paternalism can never be a recipe for entrepreneurial growth and high labour productivity. The active involvement of the majority of the Ecuadorian population in decision making and planning, and in the management of the means of production, is an essential component of socio-economic change.

Thirdly, there should be an emphasis on national self-reliance, reducing to a minimum the country's dependence upon foreign technology, technical assistance, aid and investment. Much of the production initiated by foreign investors could equally have been initiated by Ecuadorian investors, and much of the expertise provided by foreigners could just as easily be provided by Ecuadorians. Ecuador's problem for decades has not so much been shortage of resources or of expertise, as inability to mobilize resources, and lack of confidence. Of course, Ecuador would not be able to avoid substantial imports of industrial products and of agricultural and industrial raw materials, but the government could take a much more courageous hand in refusing tied aid and rejecting many foreign investments. The mobilization of internal resources is a vital step in any real development process, and too much aid may simply postpone such mobilization (see Bauer, 1966).

The suggested emphasis upon redistribution, social mobilization and self-reliance, would create an Ecuador very different from the one which will be produced by the present dependent development process. The author would be the first to admit, however, that redistribution, social mobilization and self-reliance are simply 'pies in the Ecuadorian sky'. The terms have been basic policy platforms of the 'Revolutionary Nationalist Government', but they have been pure hollow rhetoric, covering a shift towards increased internal inequalities, the growing marginalization of large sectors of the Ecuadorian population, and increased foreign dependence. It would be foolish to think that major transformations will occur in Ecuador in the near future. Many books have been written about reform and revolution in Latin America, but few have been written about continuity, reaction and the maintenance of the existing social, political and economic orders.[38] In reality, however, the forces of reaction and systemic maintenance are dominant in Ecuador, as in most other

[38] Examples of the abundant literature on reform and revolution are Burnell (1972), Petras and Zeitlin (1968), and von Lazer and Kaufman (1969). Two of the few authors who have focussed upon conservatism and stability are Mander (1972), and Veliz (1965).

Latin American countries. Observers of Latin American affairs, and particularly of events in Ecuador, have generally been too ready to believe reformist and revolutionary rhetoric, and have given too little attention to the forces which oppose real changes. In general, too much attention has been given to politicians' words, and too little has been given to the failure of official actions to match up to stated intentions.

It is to be hoped that the discussion of Ecuadorian development planning in Chapter IV has led the reader to three major conclusions: first, that planning is not taken seriously by many members of Ecuador's successive governments, and should not be taken too seriously by the astute observer; second, that planning has become an elite and technocratic exercise divorced from the real problems of the Ecuadorian population and the expression of popular aspirations; and third, that the whole planning system is essentially a dependent system, mirroring and expressing the foreign dependence of the Ecuadorian economy and society. It is probable that planning can never be very effective in small, dependent Latin American nations, because the most important decisions affecting their economies are all outside their control. Planning can only become effective if foreign dependence is reduced, and if new, more collaborative and egalitarian relationships are built with foreign advisors, financiers and governments. Furthermore, Latin American planners have often copied types and styles of planning from the more developed countries which have not even been successful in their countries of origin. The demise of planning in the more prosperous western nations such as the United States (see Catanese, 1974; Hoos, 1972) and Britain (see Bromhead, 1973; Denton, Forsyth and Maclennan, 1968, 108–32; Jewkes, 1968), should lead Ecuadorian planners towards simpler, shorter-term styles of planning. Once these have been shown to work, and the first steps in reducing the nation's foreign dependence and in developing a system of popular participation have been taken, then more sophisticated, longer-term planning styles can gradually be introduced.

In Ecuador, planning, like land reform and government programmes to help the Indian population, has usually been a masquerade to impress Ecuadorian and foreign interests. The government has generally been very half-hearted and impractical in its attitude to planning, and the few positive attempts to implement plans have been frustrated by political instability and intra-governmental rivalries. It would be unreasonable to conclude a monograph on planning without quoting from perhaps the most important study ever prepared on planning in less-developed countries; Waterston's 'Development Planning: Lessons of Experience'. More than any other author, Waterston has stressed the need for government commitment and stability, emphasizing that: 'The cardinal lesson to be learned from the planning experience of developing countries is that sustained governmental commitment is a *sine qua non* for development'. (Waterston, 1965, 340). Instead of a highly-complex planning system transplanted from the developed countries, Ecuador needs a simpler, cheaper and more rapid type of planning, playing a central role in a new, more stable and efficient governmental system. Planning is necessary to avoid wasting scarce resources on unsuitable, unnecessary and overlapping projects, and on projects which are never completed. The basic purpose of development planning should, therefore, be to choose and prepare suitable priority projects, and to ensure the continuity and completion of these projects. Particular emphasis should be given to the integration of planning with plan implementation, and to the development of local-level popular participation in decision making and project completion.

Waterston (1965, 6) has rightly commented that:

'When a country's leaders in a stable government are strongly devoted to development, inadequacies of the particular form of planning used — or even the lack of any formal planning — will not seriously impede the country's development. Conversely, in the absence of political commitment or stability, the most advanced forms of planning will not make a significant contribution towards a country's development'.

Without a major change in the attitudes and values of those in power in Ecuador, it is unlikely that planning can ever succeed, or that the benefits of economic growth will ever reach the majority of the population. It seems, therefore, that the most important of all preconditions for effective development and planning in Ecuador is a thorough internal political and social transformation leading to a reduction in the country's foreign dependence. Though such a transformation is desirable, however, there is little indication that it will occur in the near future.

BIBLIOGRAPHY

ACOSTA-SOLIS, Misael, (1959), *El noroccidente ecuatoriano*. (Quito, Instituto Ecuatoriano de Ciencias Naturales).

AGEE, Philip, (1975), *Inside the company: CIA diary*. (Harmondsworth, Penguin).

AGRAR UND HYDROTECHNIC GMBH, (1972), *Estudios hidroeconómicos de Manabí*. (Portoviejo, Centro de Rehabilitación de Manabí).

AGUIRRE BELTRAN, Gonzalo, (1967), *Regiones de refugio*. (México DF, Instituto Nacional Indigenista).

BARAONA, Rafael, (1967), 'Cambios en tenencia de la tierra y la demanda externa: algunas observaciones sobre la costa ecuatoriana'. Pp 421–8 in Centre National de la Recherche Scientifique (ed), *Les problèmes agraires des Amériques Latines*. (Paris).

BAUER, P T, (1966), 'Foreign aid: an instrument for progress ?', pp 31–58 in WARD, Barbara, and BAUER, P T. *Two views on aid to developing countries*. (London, Institute of Economic Affairs, Occasional Paper No 9).

BCE (BANCO CENTRAL DEL ECUADOR), (1971), *Boletín*. Año 45, Nos 528–30. (Quito).

BCE, (1974), *Boletín*, Año 47, no 559. (Quito).

BCE, (1975), *Información estadística*, no 1344. (Quito).

BCE, (1976a), *Información estadística*, no 1359. (Quito).

BCE, (1976b), *Información estadística*, no 1369. (Quito).

BCE, (1976c), *Cuentas nacionales del Ecuador: cifras provisionales*. (Quito).

BENALCAZAR PABON, Carlos, (1971), *La abolición del trabajo precario en la agricultura*. (Quito, Editorial Olmedo).

BONIFAZ, Emilio, (1975), *Los indígenas de altura del Ecuador*. (Quito).

BONILLA, Frank, and GIRLING, Robert, (eds), (1973), *Structures of dependency*. (East Palo Alto, Calif, Pacific Studies Center).

BOORSTEIN, Edward, (1968), *The economic transformation of Cuba*. (New York, Monthly Review Press).

BOTTOMLEY, Anthony, (1966), 'Planning in an underutilization economy: the case of Ecuador'. *Social and Economic Studies*, vol 15, pp 305–13.

BROMHEAD, Peter, (1973), *The great white elephant of Maplin Sands: the neglect of comprehensive transport planning in government decision-making*. (London, Paul Elek).

BROMLEY, R J (1972), 'Agricultural colonization in the upper Amazon basin: the impact of oil discoveries'. *Tijdschrift voor Economische en Sociale Geografie*, vol 63, pp 278–94. BROOKFIELD, Harold, (1975), *Interdependent development*. (London, Methuen).

BROWNRIGG, Leslie Ann, (1974), 'Interest groups and regime changes in Ecuador'. *Inter-American Economic Affairs*, vol 28, pp 3–17.

BURGOS GUEVARA, Hugo (1970), *Relaciones interétnicas en Riobamba*. México DF, Instituto Indigenista Interamericano, Ediciones Especiales no 55).

BURNELL, Elaine H, (ed), (1972), *One spark from holocaust: the crisis in Latin America*. (New York, Interbook Inc).

CACHO, C P, (1975), 'The road to plan implementation'. *Finance and Development*, vol 12, no 4, pp 42–6.

CALZADA, José, (1960), *Problemas del comercio del banano en el Ecuador*. (Guayaquil, Asociación Nacional de Bananeros del Ecuador).

CARDOSO, Fernando Henrique, (1972), 'Dependency and development in Latin America'. *New Left Review*, no 74, pp 83–95.

CATANESE, Anthony James, (1974), *Planners and local politics: impossible dreams*. (Beverly Hills, Calif, Sage Publications).

CHILCOTE, Ronald H, (1974), 'A critical synthesis of the dependency literature'. *Latin American Perspectives*, vol 1, no 1, pp 4–29.

CIDA (COMITE INTERAMERICANO DE DESARROLLO AGRICOLA), (1965), *Ecuador: tenencia de la tierra y desarrollo socio-económico del sector agrícola*. (Washington DC, Pan American Union).

CISNEROS CISNEROS, César, (1959), 'Indian migrations from the Andean zone of Ecuador to the lowlands'. *América Indígena*, vol 19, pp 225–31.

CLARK, Colin, (1940), *The conditions of economic progress*. (London, Macmillan).

CLOWER, Robert W, DALTON, George, HARWITZ, Mitchell, and WALTERS, A A, (1966), *Growth without development: an economic survey of Liberia*. (Evanston, Ill, Northwestern Univ Press).

CMEB (COMISION MIXTA ECUADOR–BRASIL), (1970), *La via interoceanica, la red vial del Napo, y el petroleo*. (Quito, Ministerio de Relaciones Exteriores).

COCKCROFT, James D, FRANK, André Gunder, and JOHNSON, Dale L, (1970), *Dependence and underdevelopment: Latin America's political economy*. (New York, Doubleday Anchor).

COMMITTEE OF NINE (1964), *Evaluación del Plan General de Desarrollo Económico y Social del Ecuador*. (Washington DC, Alliance for Progress).

CONFORTI, Emilio A, (1960), *Colonización, reforma agraria, migraciones internas*. (Quito, JNPC).

COTLER, Julio, (1970), 'The mechanics of internal domination and social change in Peru'. Pp 407–44 in HOROWITZ, Irving L, (ed), *Masses in Latin America*. (New York, Oxford Univ Press).

CPEO (CONSEJO PROVINCIAL DE EL ORO), (1973), *Programa de obras prioritarias, 1973–1976*. (Machala, CPEO).

CREA (CENTRO DE RECONVERSION ECONOMICA DEL AZUAY, CAÑAR Y MORONA–SANTIAGO), (1970), *Planteamientos al BID*. (Cuenca).

CUEVA, Agustín, (1972), *Notas sobre la economia ecuatoriana en la epoca colonial*. (Quito, Universidad Central, Instituto de Investigaciones Económicas y Financieras).

CUEVA, Agustín, (1973), *El proceso de dominación política en Ecuador*. (Quito, Ediciones Crítica).

DALMASSO, Etienne, and FILLON, Pierre, (1970), 'Influences comparées de Quito et Guayaquil (Equateur)'. *Bulletin de l'Association de Géographes Français*, no 382–3, pp 213–9.

DALMASSO, Etienne, and FILLON, Pierre, (1973), 'Quito et Guayaquil: aspect de l'organisation spatiale de l'Equateur'. *Cahiers des Amériques Latines*, no 7, 1ᵉʳ semestre, pp 9–34.

DELER, Jean-Paul, (1975), 'L'espace national équatorien: un modèle de structure géographique'. *L'Espace Géographique*, no 5, pp 165–75.

DELL, Sidney S, (1966), 'The early years of LAFTA's experience'. Pp 105–23 in WIONCZEK, Miguel S, (ed), *Latin American economic integration: experiences and prospects*. (New York, Praeger).

DENTON, Geoffrey, FORSYTH, Murray, and MACLENNAN, Malcolm, (1968), *Economic planning and policies in Britain, France and Germany.* (London, George Allen and Unwin).

DGEC (DIRECCION GENERAL DE ESTADISTICA Y CENSOS), (1956), *Primer censo agropecuario nacional 1954.* (Quito).

DGEC, (1960), *Primer censo de población del Ecuador 1950: resumen de características.* (Quito).

DGEC, (1964), *Segundo censo de población y primer censo de vivienda 1962.* (Quito).

DGEC, (1968a), *Proyección de la población del Ecuador 1960–1980.* (Quito).

DGEC, (1968b), *Cartografía estadística demográfica a 1962.* (Quito).

DGEC, (1969a), *Segundo censo de manufactura y minería 1965.* (Quito).

DGEC, (1969b), *Encuesta agropecuaria nacional 1968.* (Quito).

D'UGARD, Carlos, (1966), 'Experience in the Andean region'. Pp 99–122 in INTER-AMERICAN DEVELOPMENT BANK (ed), *Community development theory and practice: round table.* (Washington DC, IADB).

EFE (EMPRESA DE FERROCARRILES DEL ESTADO), (1958), *Plan general para el financiamiento y rehabilitación de los ferrocarriles ecuatorianos.* (Quito).

FISHER, Allan G B, (1945), *Economic progress and social security.* (London, Macmillan).

FRANK, André Gunder, (1971), *Capitalism and underdevelopment in Latin America.* (Harmondsworth, Penguin).

FRANK, André Gunder, (1974), 'Dependence is dead, long live dependence and the class struggle'. *Latin American Perspectives,* vol 1, no 1, pp 87–106.

FRIEDMANN, John, (1966), *Regional development policy: a case study in Venezuela.* (Cambridge, Mass, MIT Press).

FRIEDMANN, John, (1973), *Retracking America: a theory of transactive planning.* (New York, Doubleday Anchor).

GALARZA ZAVALA, Jaime, (1974), *El festin del petroleo.* (Caracas, Universidad Central de Venezuela, Facultad de Ciencias Económicas y Sociales).

GIBSON, Charles R, (1971), *Foreign trade in the economic development of small nations: the case of Ecuador.* (New York, Praeger).

GIRLING, Robert, (1973), 'Dependency, technology and development'. Pp 46–62 in BONILLA, Frank, and GIRLING, Roberts (eds), *Structures of dependency.* (East Palo Alto, Calif, Pacific Studies Center).

GMM and CPM (GOBERNACION MILITAR DE MANABI, and CONSEJO PROVINCIAL DE MANABI), (1975), *Programación sectorizada de Manabí para el trienio 1975–1976–1977.* (Portoviejo).

GONZALEZ CASANOVA, Pablo, (1969), 'Internal colonialism and national development'. Pp 118–39 in HOROWITZ, Irving L, DE CASTRO, Josué, and GERASSI, John, (eds), *Latin American radicalism.* (New York, Vintage Books).

GRIFFIN, Keith B, (1969), *Underdevelopment in Spanish America: an interpretation.* (London, George Allen and Unwin).

GRIFFIN, Keith B, and ENOS, John L, (1970), *Planning development.* (Reading, Mass, Addison-Wesley).

GRNE (GOBIERNO REVOLUCIONARIO Y NACIONALISTA DEL ECUADOR), (1972), *Filosfía y plan de acción del Gobierno Revolucionario y Nacionalista del Ecuador.* (Quito).

GRUNWALD, Joseph, (1970), 'Some reflections on Latin American industrialization policy'. *Journal of Political Economy,* vol 78, pp 826–56.

HALCROW AND PARTNERS, (1971), *Jubones River study: final report.* (London, Ministry of Overseas Development).

HECHTER, Michael, (1975), *Internal colonialism: the Celtic fringe in British national development, 1536–1966.* (London, Routledge and Kegan Paul).

HIRSCHMAN, Albert O (1958), *The strategy of economic development.* (New Haven, Conn, Yale Univ Press).

HURTADO, Osvaldo, (1969), *Dos mundos superpuestos: ensayo de diagnóstico de la realidad ecuatoriana.* (Quito, INEDES).

HURTADO, Osvaldo, and HERUDEK, Joachim, (1974), *Organización popular y desarrollo.* (Quito, INEDES).

IADB (INTER-AMERICAN DEVELOPMENT BANK), (1963), *Plan preliminar de tres años para el desarrollo de las provincias del Azuay, Cañar y Morona-Santiago.* (Washington, DC).

IADB, (1966), *Hacia un programa de integración fronteriza Colombo–Ecuatoriano.* (Washington, DC).

IADB, (1973), *Identificación de prioridades de inversión en el sector agropecuario de Ecuador.* (Washington, DC).

IADB, (1976), *Economic and social progress in Latin America: annual report 1975.* (Washington, DC).

IERAC (INSTITUTO ECUATORIANO DE REFORMA AGRARIA Y COLONIZACION), (1965), *Proyecto de colonización del Valle del Río Nangaritza.* (Quito).

IERAC, (1966), *Estudio de la realidad agropecuaria de Santo Domingo de los Colorados.* (Quito).

IERAC, (1970a), *Proyecto Palora.* (Quito).

IERAC, (1970b), *Plan de colonización de la región nor-oriente del Ecuador para 1971.* (Quito).

ILO (INTERNATIONAL LABOUR OFFICE), (1953), *Informe de la Misión conjunta de las Naciones Unidas y los Organismos Especializados para el estudio de los problemas de las publaciones indígenas andinas: tomo II.* (Geneva).

INC (INSTITUTO NACIONAL DE COLONIZACION), (1961), *Colonización del Oriente ecuatoriano.* (Quito).

INC, (1962a), *Colonización del oriente: plan vial de habilitación de tierras.* (Quito).

INC, (1962b), *Plan vial de colonización oriental.* (Quito).

INECEL (INSTITUTO ECUATORIANO DE ELECTRIFICACION) (1971), *INECEL y el Plan Nacional de Electrificación.* (Quito).

INEFOS (INSTITUTO ECUATORIANO DE FORMACION SOCIAL), (1973), *La circunstancia actual (Ecuador 1973).* (Quito, INEFOS).

INGLEDOW AND ASSOCIATES, (1970), *Investigación de las oportunidades de desarrollo económico de la cuenca del Río Guayas, Ecuador.* (Guayaquil, CEDEGE).

IRELAND, G, (1938), *Boundaries, possessions and conflicts in South America.* (Cambridge, Mass, Harvard Univ Press).

ITALCONSULT, (1963), *Elementos para la programación agropecuaria del Ecuador.* (Rome).

JEWKES, John, (1968), *The new ordeal by planning.* (London, Macmillan).

JNPC (JUNTA NACIONAL DE PLANIFICACION Y COORDINACION ECONOMICA), (1956a), *Plan nacional de electrificación.* (Quito).

JNPC, (1956b), *Azuay y Cañar: desarrollo económico, situación agraria y forestal.* (Quito).

111

JNPC, (1958), *Bases y directivas para programar el desarrollo económico del Ecuador.* (Quito).

JNPC, (1961), *Plan inmediato de desarrollo.* (Quito).

JNPC, (1962), *Plan Carchi: diagnóstico y programas sectorales.* (Quito).

JNPC, (1963), *Plan general de desarrollo económico y social del Ecuador.* (Quito).

JNPC, (1964a), *Programa de desarrollo agropecuario.* (Quito).

JNPC, (1964b), 'Una política planificada de desarrollo'. *Planificación*, no 3, pp 3–63. (Quito).

JNPC, (1966), *Ecuador: política planificada para el desarrollo.* (Quito).

JNPC, (1969a), *Programa de artesanía y pequeñas industrias 1969–1973.* (Quito).

JNPC, (1969b), *El desarrollo del Ecuador 1970–1973.* (Quito).

JNPC, (1969c), *Ecuador: bases para una estrategia de desarrollo en el contexto de la integración subregional.* (Quito).

JNPC, (1970), *Plan ecuatoriano para el desarrollo de los recursos humanos.* (Quito).

JNPC, (1971), *Plan de reconstrucción de Loja.* (Quito).

JNPC, (1972), *Plan integral de transformación y desarrollo 1973–1977.* (Quito).

JNPC, (1973a), *Guia institucional del sector público.* (Quito).

JNPC, (1973b), *Chimborazo: estudio socio-económico: resumen.* (Quito).

JNPC, (1973c), *El estrato popular urbano: informe de investigación sobre Guayaquil.* (Quito).

JNPC, (1974), *Bolívar: estudio socio-económico.* (Quito).

JNPC, (1975a), *Primer lineamiento de una propuesta para una estructura institucional de planificación regional del Ecuador.* (Quito).

JNPC, (1975b), *Regionalización del Ecuador: propuesta preliminar.* (Quito).

JNPC, (1975c), *Bases para establecer una metodología de planificación regional para el Ecuador.* (Quito).

JOHNSTON, G A, (1970), *The International Labour Organization: its work for social and economic progress.* (London, Europa Publications).

KENDALL, Sarita, (1975), 'Ecuador: oil and development'. *BOLSA Review*, vol 9, pp 316–22.

KONIG, Mechthild, (1972), *El papel de la clase media en el desarrollo económico del Ecuador.* (Bilbao, Ediciones Deusto).

KUZNETS, S, (1960), 'Economic growth of small nations'. Pp 14–32 in ROBINSON, E A G (ed), *Economic consequences of the size of nations.* (London, Macmillan).

LAHMEYER LOBO, E M, (1966), 'Evolução da idéia de planejamento econômico na América Latina'. *Jahrbuch für Geschichte von Staat, Wirtschaft und Gesellschaft Lateinamerikas*, vol 3, pp 319–401.

MCCUSKER, H F, and PODESTA, E A, (1964), *Manpower and educational planning in the socioeconomic development of Ecuador.* (Menlo Park, Calif, Stanford Research Institute).

MCGEE, T G, (1974), *The persistence of the proto-proletariat: occupational structures and planning for the future of Third World cities.* (Los Angeles, Univ of California, Los Angeles, School of Architecture and Urban Planning, Comparative Urbanization Series no 4).

MAE (MISION ANDINA DEL ECUADOR), (1970a), *Area de Pimampiro.* (Quito).

MAE, (1970b), *Pucayacu.* (Quito).

MAE, (1972), *Programas de acción inmediata.* (Quito).

MAIER, Georg, (1969a), 'The boundary dispute between Ecuador and Peru'. *American Journal of International Law,* vol 63, pp 28–46.

MAIER, Georg, (1969b), *The Ecuadorean presidential election of June 2, 1968: an analysis.* (Washington, DC, Institute for the Comparative Study of Political Systems, Election Analysis Series no 6).

MAIER, Georg, (1971), 'Presidential succession in Ecuador, 1830–1970', *Journal of Inter-American Studies and World Affairs,* vol 13, pp 475–509.

MANDER, John, (1972), *The unrevolutionary society: the power of Latin American conservatism in a changing world.* (New York, Harper and Row).

MARROQUIN, Alejandro D, (1972), *Balance del indigenismo.* (México DF, Instituto Indigenista Interamericano, Ediciones Especiales no 62).

MARTZ, John D, (1972), *Ecuador: conflicting political culture and the quest for progress.* (Boston, Allyn and Bacon).

MATTELART, Armand, (1970), 'La dependencia de los medios de comunicación de masas en Chile'. *Estudios Internacionales,* año 4, no 13, pp 124–54.

MAY, Stacy, and PLAZA, Galo, (1958), *The United Fruit Company in Latin America.* (Washington, DC, National Planning Association).

MEP (MINISTERIO DE EDUCACION PUBLICA), (1964), *Plan ecuatoriano de educación.* (Quito).

MF (MINISTERIO DE FINANZAS), (1973), *Boletin de estadística: recaudaciones efectuadas por jefaturas provinciales, no 12.* (Quito).

MONCADA SANCHEZ, José, (1973a), *El desarrollo económico y la distribución del ingreso en el caso ecuatoriano.* (Quito, JNPC).

MONCADA SANCHEZ, José, (1973b), *Pasado y presente de la planificación en el Ecuador.* (Quito, JNPC).

MOP (MINISTERIO DE OBRAS PUBLICAS), (1953), *Primer plan nacional de vialidad, 1953–1963.* (Quito).

MOP, (1964), *Segundo plan nacional de vialidad, 1964–1973.* (Quito).

MOP, (1969), *Tercer plan vial, 1969–1981.* (Quito).

MOP, (1973), *Highway program master plan.* (New York, Tippetts-Abbett-McCarthy-Stratton).

MRNE (MINISTERIO DE RECURSOS NATURALES Y ENERGETICOS), (1973), *Los nuevos contratos petroleros.* (Quito).

NAVARRO JIMENEZ, Guillermo, (1975), *La concentración de capitales en el Ecuador.* (Quito, Universidad Central, Escuela de Sociología).

OCN (OFICINA DE LOS CENSOS NACIONALES), (1974), *III censo de población y II de vivienda: resultados provisionales.* (Quito).

OCN, (1975), *Resultados anticipados por muestreo: III censo de población, II de vivienda, 1974.* (Quito).

OQUENDO, Lelia, (1968), 'La planeación regional'. *Información Mensual,* no 15, pp 26–34. (Quito, JNPC).

OQUENDO, Lelia, (1971), 'Centro y periferia en la planeación regional'. Country Paper no 1, *Sixth United Nations Inter-Regional Seminar on Regional Planning.* (Quito).

ORTIZ VILLACIS, Marcelo, (1975), *El cooperativismo, un mito de la democracia representativa.* (Quito, Imprenta Argentina, 2nd ed).

O'SHAUGHNESSY, Hugh, (1975), 'Ecuador III: oil policy under careful study'. *Financial Times,* 28th Feb.

113

PAREDES, Ricardo A, (1970), *Oro y sangre en Portovelo.* (Guayaquil, Editorial Claridad).

PAU (PAN AMERICAN UNION), (1964), *Survey for the development of the Guayas River Basin of Ecuador.* (Washington, DC).

PBQD (PARSONS, BRINCKERHOFF, QUADE AND DOUGLAS), (1964), *National transportation plan.* (Quito, JNPC and MOP).

PEÑAHERRERA DE COSTALES, Piedad, and COSTALES SAMANIEGO, Alfredo, (1971), *Historia social el Ecuador: tomo IV, reforma agraria.* (Quito, Casa de la Cultura).

PETRAS, James F, and ZEITLIN, Maurice, (eds), (1968), *Latin America: reform or revolution?* (New York, Fawcett Books).

PLAZA, Galo, (1955), *Problems of democracy in Latin America.* (Chapel Hill, NC, Univ of North Carolina Press).

PREALC (PROGRAMA REGIONAL DE EMPLEO PARA AMERICA LATINA Y EL CARIBE), (1975), *Situación y perspectivas del empleo en Ecuador.* (Santiago de Chile).

PREDESUR (PROGRAMA REGIONAL PARA EL DESARROLLO DE LA REGION SUR DEL ECUADOR), (1974), *Diagnóstico socio-económico integrado de las provincias de Loja y El Oro.* (Quito).

PREDESUR, (1975), *Proyecto de centros de desarrollo económico y social.* (Quito).

PRESTON, David A, (1963), 'Weavers and butchers: a note on the Otavalo Indians of Ecuador'. *Man,* vol 63, pp 146–8.

PRESTON, David A, (1965), 'Changes in the economic geography of banana production in Ecuador. *Transactions of the Institute of British Geographers,* no 37, pp 77–90.

QUIJANO, Anibal, (1971), *Nationalism and colonialism in Peru: a study in neo-imperialism.* (New York, Monthly Review Press).

RENS, Jef, (1965), 'Le programme des indiens des Andes'. *Tiers Monde,* vol 6, no 21, pp 41–58.

ROBINSON, E A G (ed), (1960), *Economic consequences of the size of nations.* (London, Macmillan).

ROUCEK, Joseph S, (1965), 'Ecuador in geopolitics'. *Contemporary Review,* vol 205, Fall, pp 74–82.

SALGADO, Germánico, (1970), *Ecuador y la integración económica de América Latina.* (Buenos Aires, Instituto para la Integración de América Latina).

SALVADOR, Galo, (1974), *La planificación y el desarrollo socio-económico del Ecuador.* (Quito, JNPC).

SALZ, Beate R, (1955), 'The human element in industrialization: a hypothetical case study of Ecuadorian Indians'. *Economic Development and Cultural Change,* vol 4, no 1, part 2, and *American Anthropological Association Memoir* no 85.

SANTOS ALVITE, Eduardo, (1975), *Desarrollo económico: ensayos.* (Quito, JNPC).

SCHUURMAN, F J, (1974), *Dependency theory and rural-urban migration in Latin America.* (Amsterdam, Centro de Estudios y Documentación Latinoamericana, CEDLA).

SCISP (SERVICIO COOPERATIVO INTERAMERICANO DE SALUD PUBLICA), (1961), *República del Ecuador: Encuesta Sanitaria Nacional.* (Quito).

SEERS, Dudley, (1972), 'What are we trying to measure?', *Journal of Development Studies,* vol 8, pp 21–36.

SELWYN, Percy (ed), (1975), *Development policy in small countries.* (London, Croom Helm).

STAVENHAGEN, Rodolfo, (1974), 'The future of Latin America: between underdevelopment and revolution'. *Latin American Perspectives,* vol 1, no 1, pp 124–48.

114

STERNBERG, Marvin, (1974), 'Dependency, imperialism, and the relations of production'. *Latin American Perspectives*, vol 1, no 1, pp 75–86.

TAMS (TIPPETTS–ABBETT–MCCARTHY–STRATTON), (1965), *La carretera marginal de la selva*. (New York).

TEITELBOIM, Sergio, (1970), 'Los paises del Pacífico Sur y el mar territorial'. *Estudios Internacionales*, vol 4, no 13, pp 38–59.

TORRES CAICEDO, R, (1960), *Los estratos socio-económicos del Ecuador: ensayo de cuantificación*. (Quito, JNPC).

UNCSD (UNITED NATIONS, ECONOMIC AND SOCIAL COUNCIL, COMMISSION FOR SOCIAL DEVELOPMENT), (1972), *Report on a unified approach to development analysis and planning*. (New York).

UNDESA (UNITED NATIONS, DEPARTMENT OF ECONOMIC AND SOCIAL AFFAIRS), (1975), *Statistical yearbook 1974*. (New York).

UNECLA (UNITED NATIONS ECONOMIC COMMISSION FOR LATIN AMERICA), (1954), *El desarrollo económico del Ecuador*. (México, DF).

UNECLA, (1961), 'Productividad de la agricultura ecuatoriana'. *Boletin Económico de América Latina*, vol 6, no 2, pp 69–95.

USAID (UNITED STATES AGENCY FOR INTERNATIONAL DEVELOPMENT), (1970), Land reform in Ecuador. *USAID Spring Review of Land Reform*. 2nd ed, vol 6. (Washington, DC).

USDOS (UNITED STATES DEPARTMENT OF STATE), (1966), 'Review of illegal and unscheduled changes of heads of state, 1930–1965'. *Inter-American Economic Affairs*, vol 19, no 4, pp 86–94.

VALLES, Jean-Paul, (1968), *The world market for bananas, 1964–72*. (New York, Praeger).

VANEK, Jaroslav (ed), (1975), *Self-management: economic liberation of man*. (Harmondsworth, Penguin).

VELIZ, Claudio (ed), (1965), *Obstacles to change in Latin America*. (London, Oxford Univ Press).

VERA ARRATA, Alfredo, (1972), *Historia de un triste banano*. (Guayaquil, Imprenta Abad).

VILLAVICENCIO, Manuel, (1858), *Geografía de la República del Ecuador*. (New York).

VILLAVICENCIO R, Gladys, (1973), *Relaciones interétnicas en Otavalo*. (México, DF, Instituto Indigenista Interamericano, Ediciones Especiales no 65).

VON LAZER, Arpad, and KAUFMAN, Robert R (eds), (1969), *Reform and revolution: readings in Latin American politics*. (Boston, Allyn and Bacon).

WATERSTON, Albert, (1965), *Development planning: lessons of experience*. (Baltimore, Johns Hopkins Univ Press).

WATKINS, Ralph J, (1967), *Expanding Ecuador's exports*. (New York, Praeger).

WEEKS, John, (1972), 'Employment, growth and foreign domination in underdeveloped countries'. *Review of Radical Political Economics*, vol 4, no 1, pp 59–70.

WEINSTOCK, S, (1970), 'Ethnic conceptions and relations among Otavalo Indian migrants in Quito, Ecuador'. *Anuario Indigenista*, no 30, pp 157–68.

WHITTEN, Norman E, (1965), *Class, kinship and power in an Ecuadorian town: the negroes of San Lorenzo*. (Stanford, Stanford Univ Press).

WHITTEN, Norman E, (1974), *Black frontiersmen: a South American case*. (New York, Schenkman).

WILLIAMSON, J G, (1965), 'Regional inequality and the process of national development: a description of the patterns'. *Economic Development and Cultural Change*, vol 13, no 4, part 2.

WRIGHT, Freeman J, (1970), 'The 1968 Ecuadorian Presidential campaign'. *Inter-American Economic Affairs*, vol 23, no 4, pp 81–94.

WYGARD, Edward J, (1963), *Bases para una política de fomento industrial en el Ecuador.* (Quito, JNPC).

ZOOK, D H, (1964), *Zarumilla-Marañon: the Ecuador-Peru dispute.* (New York, Bookman Associates).

ZUVEKAS, Clarence, (1968), 'The Ecuadorean economy in the 1960s'. *Business and Government Review*, vol 9, Sept–Oct, pp 11–18.

ZUVEKAS, Clarence, (1972), 'Economic planning in Ecuador: an evaluation'. *Inter-American Economic Affairs*, vol 25, no 4, pp 39–69.